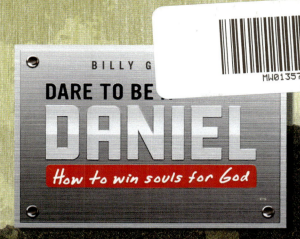

TABLE OF CONTENTS

Welcome Letter From Franklin Graham >>>>>>> ii
Purpose of the *Dare to Be a Daniel Experience* >>>>> iii
Course Overview >>>>>>>>>>>>>>>>>>>> iv
How Sessions Are Organized >>>>>>>>>>> v
Suggested Time Frames >>>>>>>>>>>>>> vi
How and When to Use >>>>>>>>>>>>>>> vii
Share and Celebrate >>>>>>>>>>>>>> viii
Discussion Tips >>>>>>>>>>>>>>>>>> ix
The Reel World Video Connection >>>>>>>>>>> x
Between Sessions >>>>>>>>>>>>>>>> xi

① DARE TO BE DIFFERENT >> 2

② DARE TO BE DISCIPLINED >> 28

③ DARE TO BE DISCERNING >> 54

④ DARE TO BE HIS DISCIPLE >> 82

⑤ DARE TO BE A WITNESS >> 108

Are we expecting too little from our kids? When it comes to God, we want our kids to learn the Bible, but are we challenging and equipping them to accomplish great things for the Kingdom? Friend, the time to train our kids to stand boldly for Jesus Christ is now.

Who has more energy and enthusiasm than elementary- and middle-school-age tweens? What if we could harness that energy for God's work and show them how they could change their world, not tomorrow, but right now—when their energy is high, their memories sharp, and their spirits bold?

Now is the time to raise up an army of young kids to take a stand for Christ and share Him with others. Give them a vision of their potential to reach others for Jesus, and with a little guidance, the discipline and drive to unleash it will follow. This **Dare to Be a Daniel Experience** will give you powerful tools to accomplish that very thing.

Sincerely,

Franklin Graham
President
Billy Graham Evangelistic Association

What's the PURPOSE of the
DARE TO BE
A DANIEL EXPERIENCE?

This five-session **Dare to Be a Daniel Experience** is based on the original 13-session Dare to Be a Daniel evangelism training course and is suitable for late elementary and middle school students ages 9–14. The purpose of this course is simple: **to inspire and equip students to effectively communicate their faith in Jesus and influence others to follow Him.**

What makes this series SPECIAL?

1. It tracks the story of Daniel, whose life account in the Bible begins when he was about the age of your students. That allows them to identify with someone who began doing big things for God at their age.
2. It uses teaching and training techniques that are proven effective for this specific age group. There are fun, hands–on activities, group work, and a plan of implementation to follow every lesson.
3. It's interactive: Your students participate. At this age, kids learn best when they are involved.
4. It's flexible: You can use this training resource for Sunday school, midweek services, youth group meetings, home groups—anywhere you want to teach and train young people to stand for Jesus Christ.
5. It involves multi-sensory learning, so today's sight-and-sound generation won't lose interest.

Why is sharing Christ so IMPORTANT?

For one thing, Jesus said so. The Great Commission—Jesus' last instruction to His followers before He left earth and returned to heaven—isn't just a request or option, but a direct command. We are called to **go** and **tell. Sharing the Gospel—the Good News about Jesus—should be a lifestyle for all of His followers, not just a responsibility for full-time ministers.** If we wait until adulthood to begin training people to actively tell others about Christ, chances are it will be too late. Now is the time—while your students are young and eager to learn—to motivate and train them to make a difference for Christ. This course will arm students with practical tools to effectively communicate their faith and influence others to follow Jesus.

COURSE OVERVIEW
Using Daniel's story, the series focuses on five key themes:

Session 1—Dare to Be DIFFERENT
Daniel *purposed* to obey God (Daniel 1:1–21).
Your students will get a glimpse of what God can do using a young person who is surrendered to Him and determined to follow His ways rather than the world's ways.

Session 2—Dare to Be DISCIPLINED
Daniel *prayed* and studied God's Word (Daniel 2:1–48).
Students will see how the powerful impact Daniel had on his world, even as a youth, was the result of his personal relationship with God. Because Daniel was devoted to prayer and God's Word, he understood God's purposes and was prepared to take a stand for God in an ungodly environment.

Session 3—Dare to Be DISCERNING
Daniel *picked* godly friends (Daniel 3:1–30).
Daniel's friends—Shadrach, Meshach, and Abednego—had already gained success and influence. But they weren't willing to compromise their commitment just to preserve their position. With their lives on the line, they refused to cave in to pressures from people and society. As a result, they had the kind of impact on their world that many of us only dream about.

Session 4—Dare to Be His DISCIPLE
Daniel *pointed* to God (Daniel 6:10–28).
Following Christ and influencing others for Him requires an authentic, active faith expressed through self-sacrifice, humble service, and uncompromising character. By considering Daniel's behavior in the face of life-threatening opposition, students will see how godly boldness and selfless humility can work together to powerfully point people to Christ.

Session 5—Dare to Be a WITNESS
(Mark 16:15; 1 Peter 3:15)
Students will review some key principles from the entire course and put together all the pieces of the Gospel presentation. By this session, the hope is that your students believe the message of Jesus is news so good they can't keep it to themselves.

HOW SESSIONS ARE ORGANIZED

Every session in this series includes:

- **Session Title**—This lets you know the main theme around which the session is built.

- **Key Focus**—This is a one-sentence summary of the direction for the session.

- **Session Overview**—This introduces the leader to the session and gives the "big picture" of what the session will cover and why it is vital for students to grasp the truths presented. This also contains a bulleted list that summarizes the key points of the session.

- **Planning and Prep**—This lists all of the props, supplies, and resources you will need for the session.

- **Jump-Start Their Hearts**—This presents two different activity options to open the session, get students involved, and focus their attention on the direction for the lesson.

- **Instant Replay**—This briefly reviews the previous session's focus and provides an opportunity for students to share their results for the "Daniel Dare" challenge from the previous week.

- **The Reel World**—This video segment typically depicts a real-life situation applying the witnessing principles presented in the lesson. This includes a small group breakout, when students will discuss how they might respond in a similar situation.

- **Xtreme Truth**—This is the main Bible lesson portion of the session, based on a particular segment from the book of Daniel. This section includes discussion and other forms of student interaction.

- **Bible in Your Brain**—This segment includes several Bible passages that support and reinforce the main Bible study. Students will have the opportunity to look up these verses and consider how they relate to the session theme and how to apply them.

- **Activity Zone**—This section contains two activity options that relate to the session topic. In a shorter session, such as a Sunday school class, there may not be time for these, but if taught as part of a weekend retreat or summer camp, these are a fun way to reinforce the lesson.

- **Witness Work**—This segment provides time to review and practice specific Bible passages and elements of the Gospel presentation that can be used when communicating the message of Christ and leading others to faith in Him.

- **The Own-Zone**—This is a time for individual reflection and consideration during which students can consider how to apply what they have learned to their own lives and situations.
- **Daniel Dare**—This is the outside-of-class challenge that students are to do on their own before reporting back the next week or next day.
- **Closing**—Each session wraps up with a closing challenge and student-led prayer.

SUGGESTED TIME FRAMES

Each Dare to Be a Daniel training session **contains over two hours** of content and options—more than most groups will be able to use in any context. That's why the general format of each session is broken up into small segments with blue directives, allowing you to **pick and choose the paragraphs, portions, questions, illustrations, etc., that are best suited to your class and time frame.** In a broader sense, the following chart provides a general idea regarding which sections to take or leave and how long to spend on each, depending on your specific time frame.

SEGMENT	45-Minute Time Frame	60-Minute Time Frame	90-Minute Time Frame
Jump-Start Their Hearts	5 minutes	5 minutes	10 minutes
Instant Replay	SKIP	5 minutes	5 minutes
The Reel World	5 minutes	5 minutes	5 minutes
Xtreme Truth	15 minutes	15 minutes	15 minutes
Bible in Your Brain	SKIP	10 minutes	15 minutes
Activity Zone	SKIP	SKIP	10 minutes
Witness Work	5 minutes	5 minutes	10 minutes
The Own-Zone	5 minutes	5 minutes	5 minutes
Daniel Dare	5 minutes	5 minutes	5 minutes
Closing	5 minutes	5 minutes	10 minutes

Teachers go to **D2BDTeacher.com** for PDFs of handouts, backgrounds for slides, promotional printables, and images. (*More student manuals can be ordered at* **BillyGraham.org/D2BD**.)

TIMESAVING TIPS

- **Each session is laid out in small segments** labeled with directives such as **EXPLAIN**, **DISCUSS**, **RECRUIT**, **REFER**, and **CHALLENGE**. This makes it easier to adapt the content to your own words and to pick and choose which segments and questions to use and which to leave out for the sake of time.

- **If discussion time is limited** (or if your students aren't inclined to respond to questions), simply turn questions into statements and use the content in parentheses following each question to further explain the issue.

- Some sections will have a red note designating which portions to use in shorter time frames.

- **Be prepared.** Have supplies laid out ahead of time and have the video cued and ready to go. All leaders involved should be aware and ready for their assigned roles.

- Review the session multiple times to familiarize yourself with all segments you intend to use.

- **Keep things moving.**

> Students go to **DaretoBeaDaniel.com** for **Daniel Logs** and other great encouragement.

HOW AND WHEN TO USE

For each session, make sure to review and choose the segments you feel will be the best use of the time you have to train your students. Don't be afraid to alter which session segments you use from lesson to lesson. Above all, pray and allow the Holy Spirit to guide you as you prepare.

Reproducibles, backgrounds for presentations, completion forms, and additional resources to help make your teaching experience a success are located at D2BDTeacher.com.

If you have multiple leaders and helpers in your group, make sure all of you have reviewed the lesson material and that everyone is clear on the key point and overall direction of the lesson. Before you present each lesson and as you prepare, ask God to show you the specific direction He wants you to take with your young people for that lesson. For your convenience, we have marked in boldface suggested text that you can read to the class.

Although this series is geared to train students to share their faith with others, it's likely you'll have youth in these sessions who have yet to receive Christ as Savior and Lord. We've built in a few opportunities to challenge those students to make that decision for Jesus. Please make sure you're ready to lead one or more of them to the Lord.

This 5-Session **Dare to Be a Daniel Experience** has been specially designed for use in a variety of contexts. In addition to more familiar contexts like Sunday school, midweek services, or small groups, **Dare to Be a Daniel can also be used as the basis for a training retreat or summer youth camp.** This training can be particularly strategic when used prior to big events or outreaches to prepare your students to lead others to Christ when they attend these events.

Be sure to visit BillyGraham.org/D2BD to order additional student Field Manuals, "Steps to Peace With God" witnessing tools, or other evangelism training resources that you may need. And if you have any questions, don't hesitate to call us at **1–888–802–D2BD (1–888–802–3223).**

God bless you for your dedication to His Gospel and the students you serve.

SHARE AND CELEBRATE

Throughout this course, you'll want to do everything possible to help your students take the concepts shared in class time and actually apply what they learned to their own lives. That's when real learning occurs. To help make this possible, the **Dare to Be a Daniel Experience** student Field Manual gives students weekly **Witness Work** and a **Daniel Dare** to do outside of class.

Every lesson then provides opportunities for you to lead your students to a time of sharing how they applied the previous session in their own lives and celebrating what God did. We call this segment **Instant Replay**, because it briefly reviews the previous session's focus and provides an opportunity for students to share their results for the **Daniel Dare** from the previous week. **Here are some helpful tips on how you can make the most of this time:**

1. **Ask which students completed the work in their D2BD student Field Manual** related to the previous lesson. Consider offering a prize (such as candy or a small trinket) to those who completed the exercises. As they share their experiences

during the **Instant Replay** segment, it will be an encouragement to the other students to participate in these weekly "on your own" experiences.

2. **Don't be too quick to correct** those who get off track in their work in or out of class. Remember that learning and growing in God is a process and we don't always do things the right way every time. The important thing is that they are learning to take what you share in class and actually do something with that knowledge on their own!

3. **Don't allow the same students** to always dominate the discussion and in the process cause more introverted students to shut down and not share.

4. **Be quick to celebrate** and give high-fives, handshakes, and hugs to those who had the courage to go out and practice witnessing and sharing their faith or to follow through with some aspect of the lesson.

DISCUSSION TIPS

Most kids love to talk, but sometimes it may seem like they're not talking at the right times. You may have battled to keep kids quiet when it's time for them to listen but then had more trouble getting the same kids to open up and participate when trying to generate class discussion. The fact is that kids want to give their opinions if they feel that they are in a safe and comfortable environment where others are listening and interested in their views. If others are listening, most people are more than willing to offer their views. When it comes to getting kids to respond and generating good discussion, the key is not what you ask—but how you ask. The following tips will help you get responses to questions and lead more lively discussions:

1. **Encourage students to verbalize their views.** Students must feel free to say what they think without feeling self-conscious. What students discover for themselves sticks with them longer than anything you tell them.

2. **Be grateful for every answer.** Students should feel appreciated for their input. If you can't always affirm their views, still affirm them as individuals willing to participate. As students feel free to say what's on their minds, they will trust you and the group (and themselves) more, creating a growth environment.

3. **Don't be satisfied with the first response to your question.** Avoid setting a question-answer-question-answer pattern. Instead, allow for several responses; then encourage the speakers to dialogue with each other. This way, you move them from merely responding to you toward conversation with each other.

4. **Keep the discussion moving.** Don't let a couple or a few students monopolize the discussion. Move on to subsequent questions.

5. **Be alert to individuals and their responses.** If a student gets interrupted, go back and invite that student to share what he or she started to say. Tactfully encourage responses from quieter, possibly very thoughtful, students.

6. **Don't be afraid of silence.** Don't jump right in and answer your own questions. Give students time to consider the question they just heard. Let them know you are comfortable with silence and willing to wait for discussion to begin. (Students also learn that you will not always "rescue" them.)

7. **Turn difficult questions back to the group.** Don't feel the need to answer every question. Use these "stumpers" to generate opinions and lively discussion. ("Good question. What do the rest of you think?") Help students examine what they believe by constantly asking for their thoughts and opinions. You will benefit by understanding where they are in their spiritual journey.

8. **Be open and willing to learn from your group.** With discretion, be honest about your spiritual struggles and victories, and let students be an encouragement to you.

THE REEL WORLD
Video Connection

Young people today expect to be entertained and to participate in learning experiences that involve a variety of media. You can't escape this. It's simply the way this generation is being raised. So for each session, we've provided you with a relevant and contemporary **Reel World** video segment that you can incorporate into each session.

The videos are aimed at capturing students' attention and provoking deeper thought. You'll often find that you can engage them in lively discussion after watching these videos. They are short, usually only two to three minutes in length. Some of the videos are dramatic, some are funny, and others are serious. But they all help to make significant points related to the sessions. Their styles are intentionally diverse so kids don't get bored with them.

A word of caution: We've intentionally geared the content and visual style of the videos provided in the **Dare to Be a Daniel Experience** to be appropriate for older tweens (ages 12–14). If you have several younger students in your class or group, you may want to preview the **Reel World** segments before class to make sure they are appropriate for your students.

Note about additional videos: There are one or two other videos per lesson provided on the DVD in addition to the **Reel World** clip. These videos can be used as introductions to the lesson or as you see fit. Some are compelling testimonies of young people whose lives have been transformed by Jesus Christ—to remind your students of the people that God is calling them to reach. Others feature encouragement from Christian athletes and other students.

BETWEEN SESSIONS

Let's be honest: What young people hear or learn in your class may not necessarily impact their lives—at least not until they apply it in everyday situations. That's why we are very intentional in giving students opportunities to actually put the lesson focus to use in their own lives throughout the week and between group sessions.

The **Witness Work** and **Daniel Dare** pages are created specifically for you to hand out and challenge your students to put into practice what you've just taught them. These pages are not only in the **D2BD student Field Manual**, but are also provided as a reproducible at **D2BDTeacher.com** that you can either email to your students (and leaders) at home or download, print, and hand out in class.

Take every opportunity to encourage and challenge your students to do the outside-of-class work. Here are some tips for getting the most out of the **Witness Work** and **Daniel Dare** segments:

1. Review them with your students as part of each session's closing.
2. Consider offering bonus points or some other incentive for each student who completes the challenge work during the week and comes to class prepared to share his or her experience with others. As students hear how their peers are taking these bold steps, they will be encouraged to step out and take the challenge as well!
3. Even if a student doesn't do the **Witness Work** and/or **Daniel Dare** following the related session, encourage him or her to go back later and take the challenge.

In addition to the session-related challenges, we have provided your young people with a contemporary website they can explore on their own: **DaretoBeaDaniel.com.**

For each lesson, we provide your students with a bonus activity that they can access on this website. These bonus activities, called **Daniel Logs,** are only accessible if the student types in a pass code, which you will give the class each session. The **Daniel Log** pass code is also printed in the student Field Manual. This same area of the website also features an online journal to help students track what God is doing in their hearts.

Be sure to encourage and remind your students during each session to go online and access the activities related to that lesson. These fun activities help drive home the point of the lesson each week. Here are some suggestions for getting the most benefit out of the **Daniel Logs:**

1. Preview the **Daniel Logs** yourself before the lesson so you know what they are.

2. Don't give away in class what's on the **Daniel Log** for that week. Young people like surprises and will want to go online to discover these bonus pages for themselves.

3. During your **Instant Replay** times in class, ask how many of your students went online to write in their journal and/or do any other activities provided.

COMPLETING THE EXPERIENCE

Once your students complete the **Dare to Be a Daniel Experience**, submit their information using the completion form provided in your kit or online at **D2BDTeacher.com**. Each student will then become a member of Team D2BD. Membership has its privileges: a personalized ID card, dog tags inscribed with Scripture verses (for use as a witnessing tool), plus access to video content on **DaretoBeaDaniel.com**.

Dare to Be Different

Key Focus: Those who dare to be different for God are destined to make a difference in the world.

SESSION OVERVIEW

The world is full of followers—people who tend to go with the flow and conform to the culture around them. Even those who think they're dancing to their own tune are typically swayed by social trends and take cues from popular opinion. This is particularly common among young people, since many are self-conscious and striving to fit in. And yet most students really want to make a difference in the world. Why is that? It's because God created each one of us with a special purpose—a purpose that will honor Him and positively affect those around us.

Your challenge in this session is to help students grasp the fact that their lives can have extraordinary meaning and purpose as they surrender to and follow God's plan for their lives. By helping your students get a vision for how God can use them to impact the world, you can inspire them to break away from the crowd of conformists, part with popularity, and fulfill their God-given destiny.

Through the life and example of Daniel, your students will get a glimpse of what God can do through a young person who is surrendered to God and determined to follow His ways rather than the world's ways. When kids are willing to stand up and stand out, God will use them in powerful ways.

Through this session, students will learn that:

- God created and saved them, not just for their own benefit, but so they can influence others for Him.
- By pursuing God and His purposes above all else, they are making a choice to be distinctly different from their culture and those who don't follow Jesus.
- As they resist pressure to conform to the world's pattern, your students will see God work through them to bring positive change to the world and to their friends.
- God intends to use them to lead others into a personal relationship with Jesus.
- Being different can make a difference!

PLANNING & PREP

For this session, you'll need:

1. Student Field Manuals (one per student)
2. Bibles (one per student)
3. A chalkboard with chalk, or marker board with dry-erase markers
4. Paper and pens/pencils for all students
5. Reproducibles for Lesson 1 from **D2BDTeacher.com**
6. *The Reel World* DVD (clip 1)
7. Modeling clay for all students
8. Music for "fashion show" and microphone for announcer
9. Several magazines, newspapers, ad fliers
10. Butcher paper or poster board, and marker or pens
11. "Steps to Peace With God" witnessing tool (one per student)

🔥 JUMP-START THEIR HEARTS
TIME: 5–10 minutes

OPTION 1: I'M A STAR!
MATERIALS NEEDED: Modeling clay

TO BEGIN, have students form pairs. Distribute clay or modeling dough to each student and ask them to quickly form a simple model of a star. Have them hold up their stars when they are finished. Ask volunteers to describe how they can tell what the images are. Now have them exchange stars with their partners, and allow one minute for everyone to transform their partners' stars into any food item or animal they choose. Then instruct students to hold their finished model in the air.

EXCLAIM, "Wow, these are really great stars! I mean, they're still stars, aren't they?" When students state that the models are definitely something other than stars, have a few individuals display their creations while volunteers try to guess what they are. Then discuss the following questions:

- **So how did our stars become something else? What happened to the clay?** (They applied pressure to the clay and molded it into something else.)

- **How is what we did to the clay similar to what people or situations can sometimes do to us?** (People and pressures around us can cause us to be something different from who we could or should be. If we're not careful, we can be molded into something much different than what God created us to be.)

Romans 12:2 says, *"Don't let the world around you squeeze you into its own mold, but let God remold your minds from within, so that you may prove in practice that the plan of God for you is good, meets all his demands and moves toward the goal of true maturity."* (Phillips)

- **In what ways does the world try to "mold" people, and how can this cause us to compromise God's plans for us?** (Cultural pressures and media messages often promote selfishness, greed, materialism, a desire for power, prideful attitudes, filthy language, improper views about sex, clothing that draws the wrong kind of attention to our bodies, relationships that aren't pleasing to God, etc. By imitating these things, we adopt beliefs and behavior that are common in the world but go against the standards in God's Word.)

- **How can we resist the pressure to conform to the world's patterns and purposes?** (Instead of conforming to beliefs and behaviors that are common to people who don't follow God, we must continually be renewed and transformed to God's way of thinking. This happens as we spend time with God in prayer, study His Word, and put the things we learn about Him into practice.)

POINT OUT how some of the most influential people in the world—those who are famous in entertainment, sports, or some other aspect of the culture—are often called "stars." Many young people look up to these stars and even try to model their lives after them.

EXPLAIN that God created us to be like a star—but not in the worldly sense. **God wants you to be a shining star that reflects His light and His love to the world. But you won't be able to do that if you allow the world to squeeze and mold you into something else. Today we'll consider someone who resisted the pressure to conform to the world's pattern. And because he did, God worked through him to influence others and bring positive change to the world.**

OPTION 2: WHAT AM I?
MATERIALS NEEDED: None

RECRUIT three volunteers, emphasizing that you are looking for actors. The more extroverted your volunteers, the better results you'll get. Have a leader or another volunteer take the three actors out of the room and give them the assignment below. Encourage them to be overly dramatic in portraying their characters and actions (sound effects are encouraged). Before each actor re-enters the room to perform a part, tell the audience what they'll see, as described below. During this exercise, the actors will be improvising one scenario while the audience believes they're acting out something completely different. One at a time, bring the actors in to play their parts:

- The first actor will be told to portray a ballet dancer, while separately you've told the audience that the actor is portraying a professional football player.

- The second actor will be told to give the impression of riding a roller coaster, while you've told the audience that the actor is portraying someone in the library.

- The third actor will pretend to be cutting down a large tree, while you've told the audience that the actor is a brain surgeon.

DISCUSS the questions below as a follow-up to this activity:

- **How does it feel to look foolish in front of your peers?**

- **Why is the thought of being different from others often difficult or uncomfortable?**

POINT OUT how important self-image is to most students. For this reason, being different or singled out can be very intimidating. Most young people don't want to stick out in an odd way. Most are looking for a place to fit in and belong.

- **Do you think most people your age want to be similar to others around them or different, and why?** (It depends on the individual, the situation, and what others around him or her are like. In general, students—whether they admit it or not—don't want to feel odd or different. They would rather belong and have things in common with others.)

- **How, why, or in what circumstances can being different be a good thing? How or why can it be a not-so-good thing?** (Being different is good if those around you are in trouble or not doing the right things. Being different can set a better example. On the other hand, being different just for the sake of being different can lead to troublesome or rebellious behavior.)

- **How does this activity illustrate how people often perceive Christians? Is this good or bad?** (Many people see Christians as different, even odd, in their beliefs and practices. This is good in that God's ways are definitely different than the world's ways, and His people should reflect those differences. Yet,

God doesn't want us to be obnoxious or contentious toward others, nor does He expect us to force His message on those who aren't ready to listen.)

Romans 12:2 says, *"Do not be conformed to this world, but be transformed by the renewal of your mind, that by testing you may discern what is the will of God, what is good and acceptable and perfect."*

EXPLAIN that most of us don't want to feel like the odd man out—different from everyone else. Yet, if we truly want to discover and fulfill the purpose for which God created us, we must resist the tendency to conform to the views and behaviors that are common in the world. These things typically go against the standards in God's Word and distract us from fulfilling His purposes.

TODAY we'll consider someone who resisted the pressure to conform to the world's pattern. And because he did, he was used by God to influence others and bring positive change to the world.

INSTANT REPLAY
TIME: 5–10 minutes

MATERIALS NEEDED: "Instant Replay Discussion Guide" (Reproducible 1.1 from D2BDTeacher.com)

DISTRIBUTE copies of the "Instant Replay Discussion Guide" for session 1. Since this is the first session, you won't have a "Daniel Dare" to discuss or any follow-up memory work. Consider using this time to allow volunteers to share past experiences in talking to others about God or spiritual issues. The following questions may help guide the discussion:

- **What fears or concerns do you have about talking to others about God?**

- **Have you ever talked to people about your faith or about Jesus? If so, what did you learn from that experience?**

- **What do you hope to learn through this course about sharing your faith in Jesus?**

THE REEL WORLD, CLIP 1, THE ONE WITH THE CLASSROOM
TIME: 5 minutes

MATERIALS NEEDED: DVD // "Reel World Discussion Guide" (Reproducible 1.2 from **D2BDTeacher.com**)

PLAY *The Reel World*, clip 1, "Dare to Be Different," which portrays a group of kids giving a substitute teacher an incredibly hard time in class. One student, Erica, tries not to go with the flow and gets confronted by her friends about it ... This provides a "close to home" introduction to this session.

After the video, discuss the following questions using the "Reel World Discussion Guide" for clip 1:

- **What do you think Erica does next? How could she explain why she didn't go along with the others? What would you have done in this situation?**

- **God wants us to stand up and stand out from the crowd, but there are good ways to do that and not–so–good ways. What's the difference?**

- **How can you tell when your differences are drawing attention to you rather than drawing attention to God?**

EXPLAIN that the group will talk about being different—but not weird different! And we're not talking in terms of style. **We don't want to be different just for the sake of being different, yet we must dare to be different in ways that can truly make a difference in people's lives. The fact is that *those who dare to be different for God are destined to make a difference in the world.***

Let's take a look at someone who wasn't afraid to be "odd for God"—though he was actually a pretty cool customer. He dared to be different, and eventually he would rock his world for God.

XTREME TRUTH

HERE WE GO
TIME: 15–25 minutes (including the main Bible reading)

MATERIALS NEEDED: "Xtreme Truth" Bible script from pages 4–5 of the student Field Manual (or Reproducible 1.3 from D2BDTeacher.com) // Music for "fashion show" // Microphone for announcer

IMPORTANT LEADER NOTE: Unless you have an extended time period, you will *not* be able to cover all of the material in this main teaching session. The segmented format with blue directives allows you to pick and choose the paragraphs, portions, questions, illustrations, etc., that are best suited to your class and time frame. The material here is not intended to be used word for word, but simply to provide direction so you can convey the content in your own style.

HAVE students locate Daniel 1:1–21 in their Bibles or on pages 4–5 in their Field Manuals (or distribute copies of the "Xtreme Truth" Bible script for session 1) so they can read along.

SELECT five students to read aloud a portion of the Bible text. Assign one person to each of the five character parts: the narrator, Daniel's friends, Daniel, Ashpenaz (the king's chief of staff), and King Nebuchadnezzar. Help the students know who reads next by calling out the parts as they come up.

Daniel 1:1-21

NARRATOR:
In the third year of the reign of Jehoiakim king of Judah, Nebuchadnezzar king of Babylon came to Jerusalem and besieged it. And the Lord gave Jehoiakim king of Judah into his hand, with some of the vessels of the house of God. And he brought them to the land of Shinar, to the house of his god, and placed the vessels in the treasury of his god.

KING NEBUCHADNEZZAR:
Then the king commanded Ashpenaz, his chief eunuch, to bring some of the people of Israel, both of the royal family and of the nobility, youths without blemish, of good appearance and skillful in all wisdom, endowed with knowledge, understanding learning, and competent to stand in the king's palace, and to teach them the literature and language of the Chaldeans. The king assigned them a daily portion of the food that the king ate, and of the wine that he drank. They were to be educated for three years, and at the end of that time they were to stand before the king.

DANIEL'S FRIENDS:
Among these were Daniel, Hananiah, Mishael, and Azariah of the tribe of Judah And the chief of the eunuchs gave them names: Daniel he called Belteshazzar, Hananiah he called Shadrach, Mishael he called Meshach, and Azariah he called Abednego.

DANIEL:
But Daniel resolved that he would not defile himself with the king's food, or with the wine that he drank. Therefore he asked the chief of the eunuchs to allow him not to defile himself.

ASHPENAZ:
And God gave Daniel favor and compassion in the sight of the chief of the eunuchs, and the chief of the eunuchs said to Daniel, "I fear my lord the king, who assigned your food and your drink; for why should he see that you were in worse condition than the youths who are of your own age? So you would endanger my head with the king."

DANIEL:
Then Daniel said to the steward whom the chief of the eunuchs had assigned over Daniel, Hananiah, Mishael, and Azariah, "Test your servants for ten days; let us be given vegetables to eat and water to drink. Then let our appearance and the appearance of the youths who eat the king's food be observed by you, and deal with your servants according to what you see."

ASHPENAZ:
So he listened to them in this matter, and tested them for ten days.

NARRATOR:
At the end of ten days it was seen that they were better in appearance and fatter in flesh than all the youths who ate the king's food. So the steward took away their food and the wine they were to drink, and gave them vegetables.

DANIEL'S FRIENDS:
As for these four youths, God gave them learning and skill in all literature and wisdom, and Daniel had understanding in all visions and dreams. At the end of the time, when the king had commanded that they should be brought in, the chief of the eunuchs brought them in before Nebuchadnezzar.

KING NEBUCHADNEZZAR:
And the king spoke with them, and among all of them none was found like Daniel, Hananiah, Mishael, and Azariah. Therefore they stood before the king.

NARRATOR:
And in every matter of wisdom and understanding about which the king inquired of them, he found them ten times better than all the magicians and enchanters that were in all his kingdom. And Daniel was there until the first year of King Cyrus.

EXPLAIN that Daniel was a teen—not much older than most of your students—when Jerusalem came under attack by King Nebuchadnezzar of Babylon. **This king took items from God's temple, along with some of the finest young men, including Daniel and three of his friends. They would learn the language and culture so they could eventually help run the government. To enter the king's service, the young men needed Babylonian citizenship. This was accomplished by giving them new names. Daniel's friends are better known by their Babylonian names: Shadrach, Meshach, and Abednego.**

- **How would you feel if you were taken from home, from everything familiar, and then deported to another country? How do you think this would affect your faith in God?** (Daniel didn't lose confidence in God and didn't think of himself as a victim. Despite all of the changes, these young men remained loyal to God.)

EMPHASIZE that regardless of our circumstances, God has a plan for each of us, just as He did for Daniel and his friends. But we must rely on God to help us stay strong and true—no matter what.

- **What do you think it means that *"Daniel resolved that he would not defile himself with the king's food, or with the wine that he drank"* (v. 8), and why did he do this?** (*Defile* means "to pollute or make dirty." By God's standards, Babylon's moral and spiritual climate was corrupt. Much of what Daniel would be taught went against God's laws and standards. Daniel wanted to steer clear of customs that might weaken his faith, such as indulging in things that would make him care more about his physical appetite than his spiritual appetite. In addition, the king's food may have been offered to idols representing false gods. To eat such food would dishonor God, and drinking wine could have dulled Daniel's mind. Daniel determined from the start not to go against what he knew to be right and true—even if it cost him his life.)

POINT OUT that people who are determined to stay faithful to God when confronted with temptation can depend on Him for strength to resist. Those who don't prepare their minds and hearts to stay true to God and His Word, however, will find it difficult to resist the world's ungodly ideas and lifestyles.

- **How did God honor the young men for their devotion to Him, and what impact did this have on the officials who supervised them?** (God gave them insight and understanding as well as favor with those in authority. When it was time for their evaluation, the king found Daniel and his friends to be wiser and more capable than anyone—including the advisers already serving the king. This was a testimony of God's power, care, and guidance in the lives of those who are faithful to Him.)

EXPLAIN that the world is full of followers—people who tend to go with the flow and conform to the culture around them. **But God is looking for leaders— people who aren't afraid to stand up and be different. God can use people like that to lead others into a relationship with Jesus.**

ASK students to consider whether they tend to be trendsetters or trend-followers. Point out that most teens, whether they realize it or not, tend to follow the trends because they want to be "in style."

RECRUIT a volunteer to show off his or her style, while another volunteer plays an announcer. Do a quick fashion show in which the stylish volunteer pretends to stroll the catwalk and the announcer takes the microphone and describes what the person is wearing. Play background music and encourage the audience to "ooh" and "aah" as the model displays his or her style.

Then discuss the following questions:

- **Who determines what's in style?** (Responses might include celebrities, media personalities, movie and TV stars, or fashion designers from New York or Paris.)

- **Who determines your personal style? Where do you get your fashion ideas?** (Most students will probably say that they choose for themselves.)

POINT OUT that most teens tend to view themselves as independent and original in their style. **But leaders in the fashion industry—who watch the younger generation intensely—understand that most people are followers. Very few kids are bold and inventive enough to set their own style. The industry calls them "edge kids." They are the teens who set the trends.**

EDGE KIDS aren't necessarily more popular, intelligent, or talented than the average kid. In fact, they're often considered odd. But they dare to do things out of the ordinary. At some point, their daring difference—something they do or wear or create—stands out enough that it begins to catch on with influential people. Suddenly, an edge kid's odd style becomes a trend that many of us follow.

- **Do you think edge kids worry about what others think when they try something new and different? Why or why not?**

CHALLENGE students to consider how cool it would be to come up with an idea that catches on around the world. Perhaps they don't see their potential for that kind of influence, but the stuff edge kids do isn't popular at first either. In fact, it may seem weird to people around them. But edge kids aren't afraid of what people think. They dare to be different.

EXPLAIN that the issue is not clothing and fashions. **God created each of us for a special purpose, and He intends for us to have influence in ways that are far more important than the latest trends. God wants you to be a spiritual edge kid—like Daniel—honoring God no matter what others think.**

- **In what ways do people often view Christians as different or even odd? Why do they have such impressions?** (Sometimes Christians give off certain impressions—good and bad—by what they say and do. But many people have preconceived notions of what it means to be a Christian.)

EXPLAIN that when we dare to take a stand for God, we not only influence people who don't know Jesus, but we also encourage those who do know Him to become bolder in their faith. **Daniel had that effect on his friends Shadrach, Meshach, and Abednego. Like Daniel, they were spiritual edge kids. They dared to be different and influenced an entire empire.**

- **What do you think God could do through you if you dared to be different in a positive, God-honoring way?** (Encourage students to dream a bit about how God could use them if they really took a bold stand and trusted Him completely.)

- **In what ways do students your age think about making a difference in the world or making it a better place?** (They'll likely mention things like taking care of the environment, helping the homeless, promoting peace, volunteering, etc. Point out that while these causes are worthy, there's an even more important way—an eternal way—to impact people's lives. We can help others see what it means to have a personal relationship with Jesus, so they can be with Him forever.)

EXPLAIN that in God's kingdom, those who make the biggest difference are willing to be different. This doesn't mean being odd or strange (although some will view Christians that way), nor does it mean being different just for the sake of being different. But as your students follow God's purposes and live by His standards, they'll think, act, and live differently from most people who don't follow Jesus.

POINT OUT that the world entices us with a lot of fine-looking things—like those set before Daniel and his friends at the king's table. We have the choice whether to take or leave what the world offers.

Matthew 6:33 says, *"But seek first the kingdom of God and his righteousness, and all these things will be added to you."* **In other words, when you put God first, He will take care of your needs and give you the fulfilling life He intends for you.**

EXPLAIN that Daniel and his friends could easily have gone along with the culture. **Some Christians think that the best way to influence people is to become more like them so they can "relate." But why would people want what we have if they don't see a positive difference from what they already have?**

1 Peter 2:11–12 says, *"Beloved, I urge you as sojourners and exiles to abstain from the passions of the flesh, which wage war against your soul. Keep your conduct among the Gentiles honorable, so that when they speak against you as evildoers, they may see your good deeds and glorify God on the day of visitation."*

- What do you think it means to live *"as sojourners and exiles"*?

- What kinds of good deeds or actions could you do that might help people see Jesus better and inspire them to trust and honor God?

EXPLAIN that Daniel understood others were watching him—and—he knew how he lived would reveal the authenticity of his faith and the power of God. **It wasn't Daniel's skills or aptitude that made him effective for God. It was his faithfulness to God through a challenging situation.**

- **From what we know about Daniel so far, what were some of the difficult and different circumstances he faced?** (He had been taken to a *different* country, immersed in a *different* culture, subjected to a *different* routine, and given a *different* name. He was in a different world altogether, facing the challenge of what he would do with his faith.)

POINT OUT how Daniel's situation is similar to the challenges students face as they proceed through middle school, junior high, and high school. Like Daniel, they have to decide whether the changes will have a positive or a negative effect on them. Daniel didn't allow the pressures and practices of the surrounding culture to change him in a negative way. Instead, he determined to change his culture in a positive way. *By daring to be different, Daniel was destined to make a difference in his world.* **As we trust Jesus and let His life show through us, we can make such a difference in the world.**

BIBLE IN YOUR BRAIN
TIME: 5–10 minutes

MATERIALS NEEDED: Bible and/or pages 6–7 in the student Field Manual (or Reproducible 1.4 from **D2BDTeacher.com**)

INVITE the students to explore what else the Bible says about the difference Jesus makes in our lives and how daring to be different for God can help influence others in a positive way. (Have volunteers read the passages one at a time. Some of these you will recognize from the main teaching time. If you have time, briefly discuss the implications of each.)

(**LEADER NOTE:** Depending on your time frame, you may want to cover only a few of these passages, as students will cover most of them in brief devotional segments in their Field Manuals.)

Romans 12:1-2
"I appeal to you therefore, brothers, by the mercies of God, to present your bodies as a living sacrifice, holy and acceptable to God, which is your spiritual worship. Do not be conformed to this world, but be transformed by the renewal of your mind, that by testing you may discern what is the will of God, what is good and acceptable and perfect."

2 Corinthians 5:17
"Therefore, if anyone is in Christ, he is a new creation. The old has passed away; behold, the new has come."

Ephesians 2:10
"For we are his workmanship, created in Christ Jesus for good works, which God prepared beforehand, that we should walk in them."

Galatians 2:20

"I have been crucified with Christ. It is no longer I who live, but Christ who lives in me. And the life I now live in the flesh I live by faith in the Son of God, who loved me and gave himself for me."

2 Corinthians 6:17-18

"Therefore go out from their midst, and be separate from them, says the Lord, and touch no unclean thing; then I will welcome you, and I will be a father to you, and you shall be sons and daughters to me, says the Lord Almighty."

1 Peter 2:11-12

"Beloved, I urge you as sojourners and exiles to abstain from the passions of the flesh, which wage war against your soul. Keep your conduct among the Gentiles honorable, so that when they speak against you as evildoers, they may see your good deeds and glorify God on the day of visitation."

Romans 1:16

"For I am not ashamed of the gospel, for it is the power of God for salvation to everyone who believes, to the Jew first and also to the Greek."

EXPLAIN that God created each of us to make a positive difference in the world. **It's not always easy to live for God while most people rebel against Him and go their own way, but if we're not ashamed to stand out for Jesus, He can use us to influence others to follow Him. Remember this: *Those who dare to be different for God are destined to make a difference in the world.***

REFER students to pages 6–7 of the Field Manual, where they will find these passages, along with a practical challenge and prayer focus for each day of the coming week.

ACTIVITY ZONE
TIME: 5–10 minutes

OPTION 1: PROMISES, PROMISES
MATERIALS NEEDED: Several magazines, newspapers, ad fliers, etc.

BRING to class several magazines, newspapers, or ad fliers. Divide into groups and give each group a few of these items. Give students a few minutes to look through the periodicals to find ads that make subtle or overt claims about how a product will enhance a person's life. For example, an ad might imply that you'll be cooler, more successful, or more attractive if you use the product. Bring students together and have volunteers describe the ad claims to the class. Then discuss the following questions:

- **What methods do these ads use to persuade people? Are they effective? Why or why not?**

- **In what ways do these kinds of ads sway people's attitudes, opinions, and behaviors?**

- **In what situations do you sometimes feel pulled or persuaded to do things you would rather not do and you know aren't right?**

EXPLAIN that outside influences, both positive and negative, tend to sway our thinking and behavior. Often, these influences come from the people we associate with every day. These influences tend to affect our relationship with God, one way or the other.

DISCUSS ways that Christians can try to persuade others to know and trust God. Point out that our actions and examples often speak louder than our words.

OPTION 2: WORDS OF WITNESS
MATERIALS NEEDED: Butcher paper or poster board // Markers or pens

DIVIDE the class into groups of no more than four students. Give each group a large piece of butcher paper or poster board, along with markers or pens. Have them write the word *WITNESS* on their papers with the letters going down the left side of the paper.

(LEADER NOTE: Since you may not have dealt in-depth yet with the concept of being a spiritual witness, have students give their general ideas regarding what a "witness" is or does. These things may or may not convey spiritual ideas.)

Instruct them to creatively think of words or phrases that start with the letters W-I-T-N-E-S-S that describe a witness. For example:

W = **W**inning our world, **W**orking with Christ, **W**hat did I see?
I = **I**n Christ, **I**mpact my world, **I**nvestigating a scene, etc.
T = **T**otally sold-out, **T**alking about Jesus, **T**elling what I know, etc.
N = **N**ot ashamed, **N**othing but the truth

After a few minutes, bring the class back together and have someone from each group report what they came up with for each letter. Briefly discuss the following questions:

- **What is a witness?** (A witness is essentially someone who tells the truth about what he or she has seen or heard regarding a particular situation or individual.)

- **What do you think it means to be a witness for Christ? How does this happen?** (It simply means that we're willing to communicate what we know personally about Jesus. It means that we willingly share the truth about Him with others. This happens not only through words, but also through attitudes, choices, and actions.)

WITNESS WORK

TIME: 10 minutes

MATERIALS NEEDED: Student Field Manual (or Reproducible 1.5, "My Story," from **D2BDTeacher.com**) // Paper and pencils // "Steps to Peace With God" witnessing tool

EXPLAIN that it's one thing to dare to be different and be willing to take a stand for Christ, but it's another to know what to say or do when people sincerely want to know about that difference. **It's crucial to know what we believe and to be able to clearly communicate our faith in Christ. That doesn't have to be difficult, but it helps to have a plan or at least have given some thought to what we might say to someone who asks why we do some things differently.**

One of the most effective and powerful tools every Christian has to influence others for God is a personal story of what God means and how He's affected his or her life.

1 John 4:14 says, *"And we have seen and testify that the Father has sent his Son to be the Savior of the world."*

- **What does it mean to testify? What is a Christian's testimony?** (It means to tell the truth about what you've seen or heard or what you know about a situation. A Christian's testimony is a personal account about his or her experience with Christ.)
- **In what ways is sharing a personal testimony helpful when communicating the message of Christ?** (Among other things it demonstrates that God is personal, and it allows the hearer to see the difference Christ can make in a life.)

DISTRIBUTE paper and pencils and have students write down responses to the following questions:

- **How has being a Christian made you different or made you better?** (If any students have not yet made the decision to follow Christ, have them describe how they think knowing God would or should affect a person's life.)

- **What is your personal "faith story" (or testimony)?** (Refer to page 8 in the student Field Manual, where they will refine their story outside of class. If they don't have manuals, use Reproducible 1.5, "My Story," from D2BDTeacher.com. For now, have them write a preliminary draft on a separate sheet.)

REMIND students that a testimony doesn't have to be dramatic. They can simply respond to the following:

1. What was my life like *before* I became a Christian?
2. What made me decide to accept Christ as Savior, and *how* did I do that? (Helpful hint: How did you hear about Christ? What did you hear about Christ? How did you respond?)
3. What difference has Jesus made in my life? How have things changed *since* I made that decision?

Students can work from these questions or—if they have very little life history before receiving Christ—they can take another simple approach to presenting their stories: *why* they are Christians, *how* they became followers of Christ, and *what* difference it makes in their lives.

POINT OUT that students will further develop and practice their testimonies in sessions to come.

HIGHLIGHT Step 1 of the "Steps to Peace With God" witnessing tool, along with the related Bible verses that they'll memorize between now and the next session.

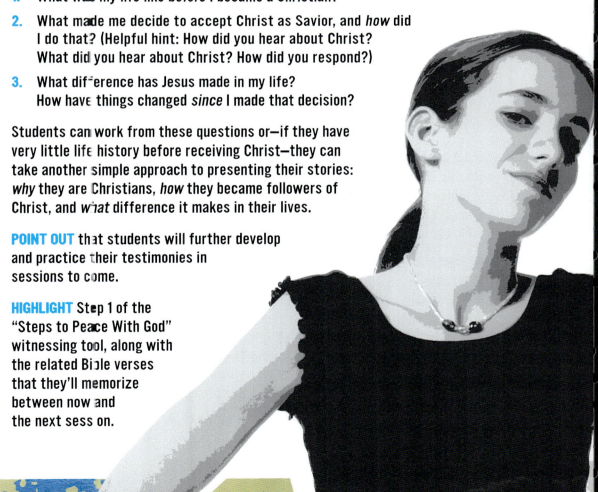

THE OWN-ZONE
TIME: 5 minutes

CHALLENGE each student to consider one of the following as it applies to their lives:

1. Is there any aspect of life in which you have not dared to be different in a way that would please God? Maybe something about your behavior isn't setting the best example or it's sending out the wrong message about being a follower of Christ.

2. Perhaps you're daring to be different and taking a bold stand for God. Now you're ready to step out and really make a difference for Jesus. Maybe you can invite some new friends to a youth event. You might even have an idea to start a new ministry.

3. Perhaps you haven't made a personal decision to follow Jesus. Maybe you come to church—even to this class—because your parents make you come or because you feel you need some "religion" in your life. But following Jesus is not about religion. Religion is about people attempting to relate to God through their own efforts or good works. On the other hand, following Jesus is about a relationship with the One who created you. If you're not experiencing this, you may want to simply ask God to reveal to your heart just how special you are and what He could do through your life to make a positive difference in the world.

ALLOW each student to find a place in your room where he or she can get alone with God and talk to Him about one of the issues above as it applies to his or her life. Challenge students to renew their commitment to take a bold stand for Christ. Encourage them to ask Jesus for help, guidance, and strength as they take the steps necessary to accomplish His plans and impact others for Him.

INVITATION OPTION: If there are students in your group who don't have a personal relationship with Jesus, invite them to trust Him today so they can become all He created them to be and make a positive difference in their world. Lead them in a short prayer, asking God to forgive them for their sins because of what Jesus did on the cross, and trusting Christ to be the Leader (Lord) of their lives. (Note: Use the sample prayer on the included "Steps to Peace With God" witnessing tool to help guide this time if needed.)

 THE DANIEL DARE
TIME: 5–10 minutes

MATERIALS NEEDED: Student Field Manual (or Reproducible 1.6, "Daniel Dare" for session 1, from **D2BDTeacher.com**)

REFER students to pages 12–13 in the Field Manual. (If they don't have manuals, distribute copies of Reproducible 1.6.) If you have extended time, students can start on this exercise; otherwise, briefly describe what they'll do outside of class.

EXPLAIN that this week they'll note several ways in which they're tempted or pressured to compromise their faith and relationship with Jesus. In these situations they must, like Daniel, make a deliberate choice not to corrupt themselves spiritually but instead to do what pleases and honors God. In each of these situations, they'll honestly describe the choice they made. In addition, they'll list ways they chose to be different from others around them in attitudes, words, decisions, and actions. Then students will describe how these choices could affect their witness for Christ and influence others in a positive way.

CHALLENGE students to come back to the next session prepared to share their experiences as they followed through on this "Daniel Dare." In the sessions ahead, they'll be equipped with tools that will help them show and explain to others the difference that Jesus can make in someone's life.

CLOSING
TIME: 5 minutes

REMIND students that God created and saved them, not just for their own benefit, but so they can reach and influence others for Him. By resisting the pressure to conform to the world's pattern, God can work through them to bring positive change and lead others into a personal relationship with Jesus. *If they dare to be different for God, they are destined to make a difference in the world.*

ASK for a volunteer to close in prayer, or lead students in the following prayer:

Dear Jesus, I thank You that I was created to know You and have a personal relationship with You. I want to help others experience that same purpose. I love You and want to obey You with all my heart, regardless of the cost. I want to take a stand for You, as Daniel and his friends did, and be willing to tell others about You. Help me make choices that will honor You and allow others to see Your work in my life. I want to be the kind of person who will inspire others to want to know You. I know I can't do this on my own. I need You to help me and to make me into the person You want me to be. I ask this in Your Name, Jesus. Amen.

DON'T FORGET the memory work, daily devotions, and "Daniel Dare" in the student Field Manual. Be prepared to share your progress in the next session.

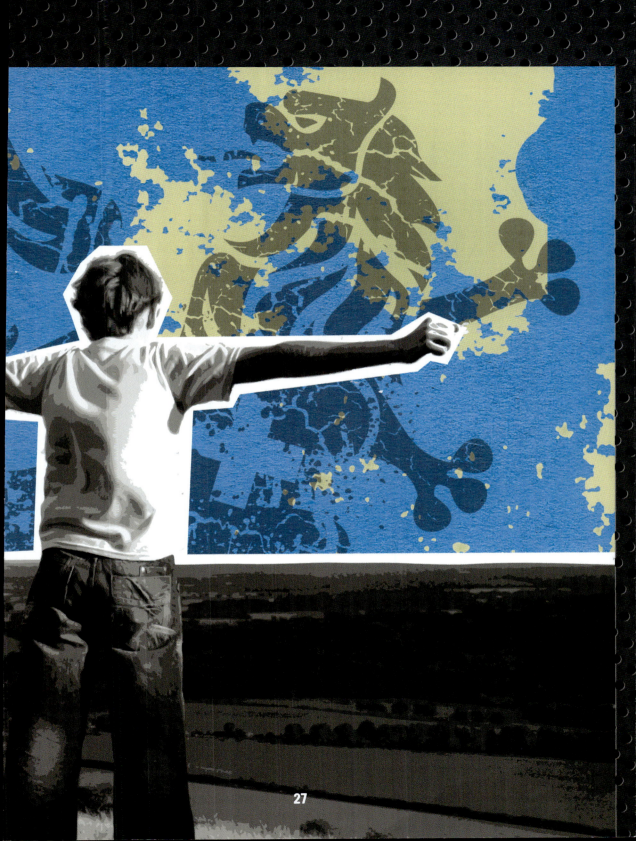

Dare to Be Disciplined

Key Focus: The better you know Jesus, the better you can help others get to know Him too.

SESSION OVERVIEW

What comes to mind when you think of discipline? For your students, discipline is probably not a pleasant thought, as it may tend to evoke images of punishment or consequences for bad behavior. As an adult, you understand the benefits of discipline, not simply as a means of behavior modification, but as it relates to developing positive life skills and habits. For Christians, discipline is a necessary aspect of discipleship—a vital part of learning to follow Jesus and becoming more like Him.

In the last session you challenged students to be different from their surrounding culture so they can have a positive impact on the world and help people see what a difference it makes to know Jesus. It's crucial for students to grasp their potential in this regard. Because they are under-challenged spiritually, many will channel their youthful energies in the wrong direction. Consequently, some will get an unfair reputation for being undisciplined. But the primary problem with unruly youngsters may not be a lack of discipline as much as it is a lack of vision. If you can help your students gain a vision of their God-given purpose and potential, then the discipline to make a difference will likely follow.

In this session, students will see how the powerful impact Daniel had on his world, even as a youth, was the result of his personal relationship with God. Because Daniel was devoted to prayer and God's Word, he understood God's purposes and was prepared to take a stand for God in an ungodly environment. As your students grasp the importance of their own personal time with God, they too will develop the core disciplines of the Christian faith that will enable them to become strong, passionate, and influential followers of Christ.

Through this session, students will learn how getting to know God through prayer and His Word can help them ...

- Grow stronger in their personal relationship with Jesus and in their ability to follow His plans.
- Realize that those who don't know Jesus are separated from their purpose and spiritually lost.
- Grasp God's purpose, share His passion, and gain His power to reach spiritually lost people.
- Become sensitive to God's guidance and know what to say when asked about their faith.
- Become more effective in helping others get to know Christ.

PLANNING & PREP

For this session, you'll need:

1. Student Field Manuals (one per student)
2. Bibles (one per student)
3. Paper and pens/pencils for all students
4. Reproducibles for Lesson 2 from **D2BDTeacher.com**
5. *The Reel World* DVD (clip 2)
6. Sheets of paper with a list of "get acquainted" questions
7. Postcards or information sheets on well-known places in the world
8. Lamp
9. One empty soft-drink can and one full, unopened soft-drink can
10. Watch with a second hand or digital display
11. "Steps to Peace With God" witnessing tool (one per student)

JUMP-START THEIR HEARTS
TIME: 5–10 minutes

OPTION 1: THAT'S MY STORY
MATERIALS NEEDED: "That's My Story" (Reproducible 2.1 from D2BDTeacher.com) or a sheet of paper with a list of "get acquainted" questions // Pens or pencils

DIVIDE the group into pairs so that each student is with someone he or she doesn't know very well. Distribute copies of "That's My Story" (Reproducible 2.1) or sheets with the following list of open-ended statements (or an assortment of your own). Allow students a few minutes to get better acquainted using this list as a guide.

- My name is … ; I have ___ brothers and ___ sisters.
- My favorite subject in school is …
- My favorite movie or TV show is …
- In my spare time, I like to …
- If I could only eat one food item for the rest of my life, it would it be …
- If I had $25,000 cash right now, I would …
- If I were a superhero, one of my goals would be …
- Someday I hope to …

AFTER students have gotten better acquainted with their partners, have each pair join with another pair and allow the students to introduce their original partner to the others by conveying two or three things they learned about him or her. Then bring the class together to discuss the following question:

- **Was it easy or hard to tell others about your partner, and why?** (It depends on how well you knew the person before. Having some topics to start with and listening attentively likely made it easier.)

EXPLAIN that if we don't know a person well, conversation can be awkward. But when we're comfortable with people, it's easy to talk with them or to introduce them to others. **That's also true of our relationship with Jesus. The better we know Him and the more time we spend listening to Him, the more comfortable and effective we'll be when we tell others about Him.**
GO TO FOLLOW-UP SECTION.

OPTION 2: WORLD REPORT
MATERIALS NEEDED: Postcards or information sheets on well-known places in the world

DISTRIBUTE to several volunteers sample postcards of famous places such as Madrid, Rome, Paris, or Hong Kong. (Or print out a sheet of information on each of the places.) Have the volunteers come to the front, and then ask them the following questions:

- Suppose you had to give a five-minute report on either this city or your favorite vacation spot. Which would be easier? Which would be more fun?

ALLOW one or two of the volunteers to give a one-minute report on one of those options. (They will likely choose to tell about their favorite place.)

POINT OUT that we can convey facts about places we've never been, but it's much easier to talk about places we really know and enjoy. The same is true when telling about a relationship with Christ.

EXPLAIN that following Jesus leads to a place far more extraordinary than any vacation destination—it leads to a home in heaven. **That's a destination we should be excited about and love telling others about. God wants us to help bring as many people as we can to heaven with us.**

FOLLOW-UP

ASK students if they've ever seen a movie, been to an event, or visited a place that they were so enthused about that they could hardly wait to tell their friends. They probably insisted that their friends go to that movie, event, or place. **That's the kind of passion Jesus wants you to have about your relationship with Him—which is infinitely more important than anything else you could see or do. If people see and hear your enthusiasm about knowing Jesus, they may want to know Him too.**

Acts 1:8 talks about being witnesses for Jesus, and 2 Timothy 1:8 talks about not being ashamed to testify about the Lord.

- **What does it mean to be a witness or to testify—like in a court?** (Witnesses tell the truth about what they've seen or heard. They testify, or tell openly, what they know about a person or situation. The more you know about the situation or person involved, the better witness you'll be.)

- **So what does it mean to be a witness for Christ or to testify about Him, and how do you become more effective at this?** (It means to tell people about your personal experience with Jesus—what He means to you and what He's done for you. *The better you know Jesus, the better you can help others get to know Him too.*)

EXPLAIN that some of us may not be as effective as we could be in our witness for Jesus because we haven't taken time to get to know Him as we should. We may know a bunch of religious facts about God and the Bible, but as we spend time with Jesus, we'll get to know Him better and become more effective at introducing Him to others.

INSTANT REPLAY
TIME: 5 minutes

MATERIALS NEEDED: Student Field Manual or "Instant Replay Discussion Guide" (Reproducible 2.2 from **D2BDTeacher.com**)

DIVIDE the class into pairs or threes. Refer to the last session's "Daniel Dare" on pages 12–13 of the student Field Manual and/or distribute copies of the "Instant Replay Discussion Guide" for session 2. Have students share with their group one way that they were tempted or pressured to compromise their faith and how they responded. Also have each student describe a situation in which he or she chose to be different in a way that could positively affect his or her witness for Christ.

XTREME TRUTH

HERE WE GO
TIME: 20—25 minutes (including the main Bible reading)

MATERIALS NEEDED: Lamp // One empty soft-drink can and one full, unopened soft-drink can // "Dream On!" script from pages 20—21 of the student Field Manual (or Reproducible 2.4 from D2BDTeacher.com)

IMPORTANT LEADER NOTE: Unless you have an extended time period, you will *not* be able to cover all of the material in this main teaching session. The segmented format with blue directives allows you to pick and choose the paragraphs, portions, questions, illustrations, etc., that are best suited to your class and time frame. The material here is not intended to be used word for word, but simply to provide direction so you can convey the content in your own style.

DISPLAY a table lamp and ask students to describe how it works and explain its purpose. Obviously, it provides light, as long as it has a bulb and is plugged in. Then ask the following question:

- **How is this lamp like a Christian?** (Christians are to provide spiritual light to those around them. But in order to fulfill that function, they must be connected to the power source.)

Matthew 5: 14-16 says, *"You are the light of the world. A city set on a hill cannot be hidden. Nor do people light a lamp and put it under a basket, but on a stand, and it gives light to all in the house. In the same way, let your light shine before others, so that they may see your good works and give glory to your Father who is in heaven."*

- **As Christians, what kind of light should we provide, and how?** (It's the light of God's truth and love. By actions, words, and attitudes, we are to reflect Christ's character so others can see what He's like. By example, our lives should illuminate the way to Jesus.)

- **What is our "power source," and how do we stay connected?** (God—by His Holy Spirit—is our Source. Those who receive God's forgiveness and enter a personal relationship with Him can stay connected to Him through prayer, reading His Word, and following His purpose for our lives.)

Psalm 119:105 says, *"Your word is a lamp to my feet and a light to my path."*

- **In what way is God's Word like a lamp or a light to our lives?**

EXPLAIN that in the last session we considered how Daniel's devotion to God gave him the discipline and determination to stand out in a positive way from the culture around him. **In this session, we'll consider how Daniel developed his boldness and strength. We'll see how spending time in prayer and God's Word can provide power, guidance, and positive influence on others.**

DANIEL 2:1—48: Have students locate this passage in their Bibles so they can refer to it during the lesson.

EXPLAIN that you're going to tell each other the story of an amazing feat from the book of Daniel, but in a slightly different style than they see in the Bible.

DISTRIBUTE copies of the "Dream On!" script (Reproducible 2.4 from D2BDTeacher.com) to six volunteers. The script is also located on pages 20—21 of the student Field Manual. Assign one of the following roles to each volunteer:

- **DANIEL**

- **NEBUCHADNEZZAR**

- **KING'S ADVISERS**

- **KING'S MAGICIANS**

- **SHADRACH, MESHACH, AND ABEDNEGO**
  (you could have three read this part together)

- **NARRATOR**

Dream On!

(Point to readers separately if they need cues when it's their turn so you can keep things moving. The reading itself should take between three and four minutes.)

NARRATOR:
Our story begins in ancient Babylon, in the court of an angry king.

NEBUCHADNEZZAR:
Who are you? Another reporter? Get lost! I need my magicians and advisers!

KING'S MAGICIANS:
O king, live forever! You called?

KING'S ADVISERS:
O king, live forever! What's up?

NEBUCHADNEZZAR:
I haven't been sleeping well at night. I have this dream that keeps bothering me. You need to help. I pay you the big shekels to do your magic stuff and to give me good advice. Tell me what this dream means, OK?

KING'S ADVISERS:
Absolutely! A few details, and we'll figure it all out.

NEBUCHADNEZZAR:
That won't happen. Earn your keep. No details, no hints. You tell me what my dream is, and then you tell me what it means.

KING'S MAGICIANS:
We can give you a sleeping potion. We can prescribe a warm bubble bath. But no one can do what you want, O king!

KING'S ADVISERS:
We can tell you where your parents went wrong in raising you. We can recommend a change in scenery. But tell you your own dream? No one's that smart, O king!

NEBUCHADNEZZAR:
Why should I leave you on staff, then? Reporter!

NARRATOR:
I'm the narrator, sir.

NEBUCHADNEZZAR:
Whatever! Write down this decree! "Because the royal magicians and advisers aren't earning their keep, they die!"

NARRATOR:
And so it was. The king's head hatchet man was sent out to kill the royal wise guys, including Daniel, Shadrach, Meshach, and Abednego.

SHADRACH, MESHACH, ABEDNEGO:
And we didn't even know what was going on.

DANIEL:
But I found out in time to ask my buddies to pray. We asked God to deliver us from death. We needed some inside information.

NEBUCHADNEZZAR:
Like from the inside of my head.

SHADRACH, MESHACH, ABEDNEGO:
Amazing feats take God's strength. So we prayed. And God really delivered!

NEBUCHADNEZZAR:
Daniel! Why do you still have your head? Are you the one who can tell me my dream and what it means?

DANIEL:
No adviser could ever do that, O king. But there is a God who reveals those mysteries, and He revealed them to me.

NARRATOR:
Daniel told the king about his dream.

NEBUCHADNEZZAR:
It all checked out.

SHADRACH, MESHACH, ABEDNEGO:
Daniel told the king what his dream meant.

NEBUCHADNEZZAR:
All about my kingdom—and future empires. Overwhelming, but very cool!

NARRATOR:
Daniel was rewarded richly.

DANIEL:
I told the king the great God had made it all happen.

SHADRACH, MESHACH, ABEDNEGO:
God gave us a promotion!

KING'S MAGICIANS, KING'S ADVISERS:
Yo, we got to keep our heads!

NEBUCHADNEZZAR:
I need to sleep at night!

NARRATOR:
So everyone got to dream for another day, thanks to God and His good servant Daniel. And the important thing to remember about this is ...

EVERYONE:
God is the God of all gods and the Lord of kings and the revealer of mysteries—and Daniel's amazing feat proves it!

THE END

CONGRATULATE students for a job well done.

EXPLAIN that dreams were a big deal in Daniel's time. Many people viewed them as a form of divine communication. That's probably why Nebuchadnezzar was frustrated when none of his advisers could tell what his dream meant.

POINT OUT that the Bible shows that dreams could be a message from God. But Daniel and his friends relied on a more practical way to hear how God wanted them to respond to the situation.

- **Looking back at Daniel 2:16–19, why did Daniel ask for time before he interpreted the dream?** (He wanted to pray for God's help. He even enlisted his friends to pray. They knew that only God could provide the answer.)

EXPLAIN that when Daniel and his friends saw the opportunity to make a life-or-death difference, they prayed and trusted God. When He answered, they gave Him glory. As a result, they influenced a king and he rewarded them. **Because Daniel was humble, open, and honest, the king recognized God's power in his life. As a result, the king gave Daniel authority over the entire province of Babylon.**

- **What should we do when God gives us the answers and the power we need?** (Responses could range from "Be sure to give God credit" to "Use the power the way God wants you to!" Like Daniel, we must be quick to praise God for His help and answered prayer.)

READ or have a volunteer read Daniel 6:3–10, while the class follows along.

- **According to this passage, what set Daniel apart from others, and why do you think he was like this?** (He was completely trustworthy and not corrupt or negligent in anything he did [v. 4]. This was a reflection of his devotion to God. Doing our best is one way to honor God.)

- **How did Daniel respond to the king's decree, and what does this reveal about Daniel's devotion to God?** (He immediately went to God for help. Though Daniel was loyal in serving King Darius, the king's order did not take priority over God. Daniel realized the danger but didn't let anything keep him from his time with God.)

POINT OUT that the title of this session is "Dare to Be Disciplined." Then ask students to describe what it means to be disciplined. Allow for responses.

EXPLAIN that *Webster's Dictionary* provides this definition of *discipline*: "training to improve strength or self-control." **Discipline implies showing integrity and sticking to a purpose, even if it's easier not to do so. When we talk about a personal discipline, we're referring to a character-building activity, practice, or habit that may not always be convenient, but it can make us stronger in the end.**

READ or have a volunteer read Daniel 9:1–4, while the class follows along.

- **In this passage, what spiritual disciplines are evident in Daniel's life, and how did these practices affect him?** (He was devoted to prayer, he knew God's Word—obviously from spending time in it—and he obeyed God. These disciplines gave him insight that others didn't have, as well as confidence, peace, and boldness in difficult situations. It was clear that God was his Source.)

ILLUSTRATION: Display two soft-drink cans—one empty and the other full and unopened. Have a volunteer take the empty can and attempt to crush it. (He or she should be able to do so with ease.) Now ask the volunteer to crush the unopened can. (Don't let the person strain or get injured. Only allow enough effort to illustrate the following question.) **Why was the empty can easy to crush, but the full one nearly impossible to crush?** (The pressure of the liquid inside resists the outside force.)

- **Why is it important to "fill up" spiritually, and how can we do this?** (If we're spiritually empty, we'll easily cave in to outside pressure. But we can hold up under pressure and win the battle against temptation by remaining full of God's presence and power. This requires listening to God through prayer and learning about Him through His Word.)

- **Why is spending time in prayer and God's Word absolutely vital in getting to know Jesus better?** (Just like in any relationship, there must be open and constant communication for the relationship to grow and stay healthy. In addition, God's Word—the Bible—is the way He's chosen to reveal Himself and His plans for us.)

- **How can getting to know God affect our attitudes and views toward others, particularly those who don't know Jesus personally?**

THE PURPOSE of this course is to learn how to tell others about Jesus. As we get to know God better, we'll understand His plans and relate to His passion for people. We'll begin to see them as He sees them, and we'll gain a greater desire to reach out with His message and love. *The better we know Jesus, the easier it is to introduce others to Him.*

LISTEN to how the following passages sum up Jesus' mission and purpose:

1 Timothy 1:15
"The saying is trustworthy and deserving of full acceptance, that Christ Jesus came into the world to save sinners, of whom I am the foremost."

Luke 19:10
"For the Son of Man [Jesus] came to seek and to save the lost."

- **What or who are the "lost"?** (Those who haven't asked Jesus to be their Lord and Savior—the Forgiver of their sins and Leader of their lives—are spiritually lost.)

- **In what way are those who don't know Jesus lost?** (People who haven't accepted God's forgiveness and entrusted their lives to Christ are missing the primary relationship for which they were created. They are spiritually separated from God and won't go to heaven. Apart from Christ, they won't discover God's ultimate plan or experience complete fulfillment.)

EXPLAIN that someone who is lost has gotten "off course." God has created each of us with a purpose that will honor Him and allow us to make a positive difference in the world. Our lives have the most meaning, significance, and joy when we follow God's plan. God gave us a free will to make that choice. But ever since the beginning, people have chosen their own way instead of God's. That's part of what it means that we are sinners. Our sin separates us from God and His perfect purpose.

- **Why is it important to recognize the fact that people are spiritually lost?** (Unless we're convinced and concerned that people are spiritually lost, we'll do little or nothing to help them find their way home to God.)

40

EXPLAIN that the heart of Jesus' earthly mission was to reach spiritually lost people. As Jesus' followers, this must be the core of our mission too. We must see people from God's perspective.

Matthew 9:36-38 says, *"When [Jesus] saw the crowds, he had compassion for them, because they were harassed and helpless, like sheep without a shepherd. Then he said to his disciples, 'The harvest is plentiful, but the laborers are few; therefore pray earnestly to the Lord of the harvest to send out laborers into his harvest.'"*

- **What was Jesus' attitude toward lost people, and what does this mean for us?** (He has compassion for them because they are helpless apart from Him. Jesus asks His followers to pray and be prepared to reach out and help lead them into a personal relationship with Him.)

EXPLAIN that other religions represent people's ideas and attempts to relate to God through their own efforts. But the Good News of Jesus is that God came to us and made the way for us to relate to Him. True Christianity isn't about religion; it's about a relationship with the One who created us to be with Him forever.

In John 14:6 Jesus answered, *"I am the way, and the truth, and the life. No one comes to the Father except through me."*

EXPLAIN that it's not popular in today's world to claim that there's only one way to God, but that's not our own idea. This is Jesus' claim as we have it in the Bible—the most scrutinized, time-tested, and proven book of all time. **No prophecy in the Bible has ever failed to come to pass how and when the Bible said it would. And no other religious leader has proven his or her claims by rising from the dead—with witnesses to back that up. No one other than God's perfect Son could have paid the price for our offenses against God and opened the way for a renewed relationship with Him.**

1 Timothy 2:3-5 says, *"This is good, and it is pleasing in the sight of God our Savior, who desires all people to be saved and to come to the knowledge of the truth. For there is one God, and there is one mediator between God and men, the man Christ Jesus."*

- **What does this verse say about God's desire for people?** (He doesn't want them to be eternally lost. He wants them to turn from their sins and come to know the truth about Jesus so they can be forgiven and have a personal and eternal relationship with God.)

- **What role can we play in helping spiritually lost people find a relationship with Jesus?**

REMEMBER the lamp. We can help spiritually lost people find the way out of the darkness caused by sin, and we can light the way to Jesus by living in a way that reflects His love and shows people what He's like. We must also be ready to tell people about the difference Jesus makes in our lives and how He can give them ultimate peace and purpose in their lives, as well. It all begins by knowing Jesus ourselves. *The better we know Jesus, the better we can help others get to know Him too.*

NARROW YOUR FOCUS
Being disciplined isn't about pushing yourself to do everything you can possibly do or managing your schedule to fit more things in. Often, real discipline means limiting your options and narrowing your focus so that whatever you do, you can do it well.

1 Corinthians 9:24-25: *"Do you not know that in a race all the runners run, but only one receives the prize? So run that you may obtain it. Every athlete exercises self-control in all things. They do it to receive a perishable wreath, but we an imperishable."*

Philippians 3:12-14 : *"Not that I have already obtained this or am already perfect, but I press on to make it my own, because Christ Jesus has made me his own. Brothers, I do not consider that I have made it my own. But one thing I do: forgetting what lies behind and straining forward to what lies ahead, I press on toward the goal for the prize of the upward call of God in Christ Jesus."*

As followers of Jesus, we need to stay focused on what really matters—something far more important than a championship trophy or gold medal. We have to focus on God and His kingdom first, knowing that everything else we need will follow.

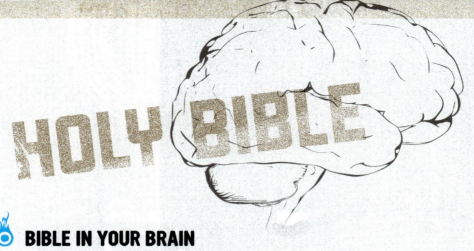

BIBLE IN YOUR BRAIN
TIME: 5–10 minutes

MATERIALS NEEDED: Bibles and/or pages 22–23 in the student Field Manual (or Reproducible 2.5 from D2BDTeacher.com)

INVITE students to look at what else the Bible says about God's love for people, His desire for us to know Him, and His plans to reach those who don't have a personal relationship with Jesus.

(LEADER NOTE: Depending on your time frame, you may want to cover only a few of these passages, as students will cover most of them in brief devotional segments in their Field Manuals.)

1 Timothy 2:3-5
"This is good, and it is pleasing in the sight of God our Savior, who desires all people to be saved and to come to the knowledge of the truth. For there is one God, and there is one mediator between God and men, the man Christ Jesus."

Luke 10:27
"And he answered, 'You shall love the Lord your God with all your heart and with all your soul and with all your strength and with all your mind, and your neighbor as yourself.'"

John 17:3
"And this is eternal life, that they know you the only true God, and Jesus Christ whom you have sent."

Luke 19:10
"For the Son of Man [Jesus] came to seek and to save the lost."

Matthew 9:35-38

"And Jesus went throughout all the cities and villages, teaching in their synagogues and proclaiming the gospel of the kingdom and healing every disease and every affliction. When he saw the crowds, he had compassion for them, because they were harassed and helpless, like sheep without a shepherd. Then he said to his disciples, 'The harvest is plentiful, but the laborers are few; therefore pray earnestly to the Lord of the harvest to send out laborers into his harvest.'"

John 14:6

"Jesus said to him, 'I am the way, and the truth, and the life. No one comes to the Father except through me.'"

1 Timothy 1:15

"The saying is trustworthy and deserving of full acceptance, that Christ Jesus came into the world to save sinners."

EXPLAIN that Jesus left no question about why He came to earth, and He intends for us to carry on His mission to reach those who are spiritually lost. In order to do this effectively, we must have a close personal relationship with Jesus.

REFER students to pages 22–23 of the Field Manual, where they will find these passages, along with a practical challenge and prayer focus for each day of the coming week.

ACTIVITY ZONE
TIME: 5–10 minutes (Optional, depending on the session time frame)

OPTION 1: PRAYER LINE
MATERIALS NEEDED: Watch with second hand or digital display

TO BEGIN, have students stand and form two parallel rows, one directly in front of the other, facing the same direction, with an equal number in each row. Ask those in the back row to place both hands on the shoulders of the person in front of them. (Align girls with girls and guys with guys if you feel that this would make students more comfortable.) Make sure the person in the back line knows the name of the person in front of him or her.

ASK those in the back line to pray silently for one minute, simply asking God to bless the person in front of them. If during their quiet time they sense any specific ideas, thoughts, or direction on how to pray, that's fine, but the only directions are simply to ask God to bless their friend. After 60 seconds of silent prayer, have the person in the back pray out loud for the person in front. Give them 45 seconds to pray out loud however they feel God directing them. After 45 seconds, have both lines do an "about face" so that those who prayed will now receive prayer. Repeat the exercise as described above. Then ask the following questions:

- **How many of you, when praying silently for the person in front of you, felt like God gave you some sort of specific direction about how to pray?** (Have students raise their hands if this was the case. A number will likely respond.)

- **How many of you, as you were receiving prayer, heard something that in some way hit on an issue in your life or was something you needed prayer for?** (Several hands are likely to go up.)

POINT OUT that this exercise is a hands-on example of how to "intercede"—to pray for others' situations, needs, and concerns. Hopefully, it also gave your students an opportunity to understand what it feels like to listen and "hear" God's voice giving them subtle but specific direction on how to pray for another person. For some, this may be an amazing revelation!

REMIND students that prayer involves listening to God as well as talking to Him—and we should spend more time listening than talking.

OPTION 2: COMMUNICATION ILLUSTRATION
MATERIALS NEEDED: "Communication Illustration" (Reproducible 2.6 from
D2BDTeacher.com) // Paper and pens or pencils

DIVIDE the class into pairs and give one student in each group a copy of the
"Communication Illustration" sheet (Reproducible 2.6). *Do not* let their partners see
what's on the sheet. Give the other partner in the group a blank sheet of paper and a
pencil. The students with the blank sheet will attempt to draw three images contained
on the "Communication Illustration" sheet through limited communication with
their partners, who will be giving clues based on the illustrations. Give the following
instructions to the person providing the clues:

- **Without talking, gesturing, or moving in any way, try to convey to your partner
  how to draw image No. 1. Go!** (Students will be confused; it's impossible to convey
  the image without doing something. After a few seconds, proceed with the next
  instruction.)

- **This time, your partner can ask questions about the image that can only be
  answered with "yes" or "no." Other than that, give no other clue as your partner
  attempts to draw image No. 2.** (Give students a couple minutes.)

- **Finally, describe to your partner what to draw for image No. 3 using any means of
  communication necessary, other than actually showing the picture.** (Most will be
  able to draw the image with a fair amount of accuracy.)

DISCUSS these questions as a follow-up to this activity:

- **Why were the first couple of attempts to draw difficult?** (The drawing was tough to
  complete when the partner who could see the picture wasn't allowed to say anything.)

- **When did it get easier to draw the image?** (When the partner who could see the
  picture was allowed to communicate openly.)

- **What is the difference between communication and simply talking?** (Communication
  implies a two-way interaction: giving and receiving, talking and listening.)

EXPLAIN that if communication is a two-way street, the most crucial part of
communicating with God is not just what we say to Him, but what He says to us.
We must learn to listen to God in prayer.

THE REEL WORLD, CLIP 2, THE ONE WITH THE BIBLE

TIME: 15 minutes (including group break-outs and follow-up)

MATERIALS NEEDED: "Reel World Discussion Guide" (Reproducible 2.3 from **D2BDTeacher.com**)

PLAY *The Reel World*, clip 2, "Dare to Be Disciplined," which shows a young man, Asa, voicing his desire to spend some time with God each night. But shortly into his time, the phone rings, he receives an instant message, and a video chat ensues ... What to do?

Though we aren't making many golden calves in this day and age, there are a myriad of things that compete for our devotion to God.

After the video, discuss some of the following questions using the "Reel World Discussion Guide" for clip 2:

- **What advice would you give Asa for tomorrow night if he tries again?**

- **What are some things that almost always seem to get in the way of your time with God?**

- **How can spending personal time with God affect your ability to influence others for Jesus?** (The better you know Jesus, the more effectively you can make Him known.)

- **Why is it sometimes so hard to read the Bible and spend quiet time with God? What would make it easier for you?**

 **WITNESS WORK**

TIME: 10 minutes

MATERIALS NEEDED: Student Field Manual // Pens or pencils // "Steps to Peace With God" witnessing tool

INSTRUCT students turn to the "My Story" exercise on page 8 in their Field Manuals so they can refer to the personal "faith stories" or testimonies they've worked on since the last session. Then have students form pairs so they can practice telling their stories to one another. Each student should take only about three or four minutes to give a concise testimony.

AFTER each person has shared his or her story, allow his or her partner to offer constructive criticism. Encourage them not to be critical of the individual's experiences, but to give input regarding what parts of the testimony were clear or unclear and how they feel it would connect with someone who doesn't know Jesus. Based on this input, students should make notes in the "My Story" section of the Field Manual so they can make adjustments next time they practice telling their stories.

If you have an extended time, refer to some of the "Testimony Tips" on pages 25–26 in the student Field Manual. These include several helpful hints, as well as some do's and don'ts that will help students tell their stories and present Jesus' message more effectively.

HIGHLIGHT Step 2 of the "Steps to Peace With God" witnessing tool, along with the related Bible verses that they'll memorize between now and the next session.

THE OWN-ZONE

TIME: 5 minutes

MATERIALS NEEDED: Pens or pencils and slips of paper or notecards

DISTRIBUTE pens or pencils and slips of paper or notecards. Have students write the names of three friends who don't know Jesus. Then ask them to cross out two of the names. While this may be difficult for some, encourage them to go along with your instructions for now. Then ask:

- **What would you say if I told you that you've just made a decision that could affect which of your friends goes to heaven and which ones end up in hell?**

   (Students may protest that they were just following instructions and this exercise has nothing to do with determining where our friends will spend eternity.)

CHALLENGE students that while we can't ultimately determine where our friends will spend eternity, we may have more influence on their decisions than we realize. This exercise may have no bearing on whether or not our friends receive Christ. And yet, if we do nothing to reach them, it can be like crossing them off the list. Of course, our friends might come to Christ apart from our influence, but if we want to be part of the process, we must start by reaching out to at least one.

EXPLAIN that Jesus doesn't intend for us to be motivated by guilt when it comes to reaching people with His message. God already wants to save people and is ready to provide opportunities if we're ready to reach out. He will empower us to lead friends to Christ if we simply obey Him.

ALLOW students a moment to pray for the friends on their list, asking God for opportunities to help these individuals find a personal relationship with Jesus.

THE DANIEL DARE

TIME: 5–10 minutes

MATERIALS NEEDED: Student Field Manual (or Reproducible 2.7, "Daniel Dare" for session 2, from **D2BDTeacher.com**)

REFER students to pages 30–31 in the Field Manual. (If they don't have manuals, distribute copies of Reproducible 2.7.) If you have an extended time, students can start on this exercise now; otherwise, briefly describe what they'll do outside of class.

EXPLAIN that if we don't set aside a specific time to spend with God each day, chances are we will never follow through. **Our lives are so busy that it's easy to forget to spend time with God until we think everything else is out of the way. But we must make our personal time with God our top priority if we really want to have His power and follow His purpose for our lives.**

ALLOW students a moment to consider the challenge in the Field Manual regarding the time they've decided to set aside each day to spend with God in prayer and reading His Word.

CHALLENGE students to come back to the next session prepared to share about the time they've determined to set aside for God and how they followed through on their commitment.

REMIND students that spending time with God must become a driving desire, not just something to cross off our daily to-do list. Our willingness to show and tell others about Jesus is directly connected to how much time we spend in prayer and studying the Bible.

CLOSING

TIME: 5 minutes

MATERIALS NEEDED: Student Field Manual

REMIND students of the sober fact that apart from a personal relationship with Jesus, people are spiritually lost and on their way to hell. But Jesus gives those who follow Him the privilege and responsibility of bringing His Good News of hope, forgiveness, and eternal life to those who don't yet know Him. **In order to fulfill that responsibility, we must spend time getting to know Jesus ourselves. As we consistently pray, learn God's Word, and put the Word into practice, we gain the insight and ability to effectively introduce Jesus to others.** *The better we know Jesus, the better we can help others get to know Him too.*

ENCOURAGE students to start praying specifically for three people they know who don't have a personal relationship with Jesus. They'll list these individuals on page 34 in their student Field Manuals. In the days and weeks ahead, they should look for opportunities to build relationships and have meaningful conversations with these individuals, in hopes of eventually leading them to Christ.

ASK for a volunteer or two to close in prayer, or lead students in the following prayer:

Dear Jesus, I thank You for not only saving me, but also for being my best friend. Thanks for the opportunity to grow in my relationship with You as I spend time talking to You and learning from Your Word. Help me develop the discipline I need to study the Bible effectively and to apply what I learn to my life each day. As I get to know You better, teach me to see people the way You see them and to reach out with compassion to those who still don't know You or the ultimate purpose You have for them. As I stay connected to You as my power source, let me be a light that clearly reflects Your character and shines the way for others to find You. I ask this in Your Name, Jesus. Amen.

DON'T FORGET the memory work, daily devotions, and "Daniel Dare" in the student Field Manual. Be prepared to share your progress in the next session.

Dare to Be Discerning

Key Focus: The ability to endure tough challenges and influence others for Christ hinges on commitment, character, companionships, and choices.

SESSION OVERVIEW

If your students' faith has not yet been tested during the course of their young lives, it most certainly will be in the days and years ahead—perhaps in ways you've never experienced. So what will they do when people challenge their beliefs and attack their values? Will their commitment to God collapse, or will they stand strong? It all depends on the strength of their character and commitment to Christ. As a leader, you can make a significant contribution to your students' faith and character development by helping them understand the benefits of bold choices and godly friendships. By surrounding themselves with positive influences, they'll more likely be inspired to make daring decisions that propel them to new heights of faith and a greater depth of devotion to God.

This session highlights the experience of three of Daniel's friends—Shadrach, Meshach, and Abednego—whose devotion to God was tested to the extreme, yet they passed the test. Because of their faith and character, they had already gained success and influence, but they weren't willing to compromise their commitment just to preserve their positions. With their lives on the line, they entrusted themselves to God, refusing to cave in to pressures from people and society. As a result, they had the kind of impact on their world that many of us only dream about.

Through this session, students will learn how:

- Relying on God provides uncommon insight and spiritual strength.
- Developing godly character gives credibility to their Christian witness.
- Their friendships impact their identity, inspiration, and influence for Christ.
- Their choices can reflect their devotion to Christ and affect their witness for Him.
- Effectively influencing others for Christ may require some relationship and lifestyle changes.

PLANNING & PREP

For this session, you'll need:

1. Student Field Manuals (one per student)
2. Bibles (one per student)
3. Paper and pens/pencils for all students
4. Reproducibles for Lesson 3 from **D2BDTeacher.com**
5. *The Reel World* DVD (clip 3)
6. An inflated balloon for each student
7. Two sets of dominoes
8. Assorted items for cast of characters in the Bible reading (see pages 63–64)
9. Jewelry item with a diamond, or photo of a diamond
10. Board and chalk or markers
11. Long rope with strip of cloth tied at the middle, and tape to mark a line
12. "Steps to Peace With God" witnessing tool (one per student)

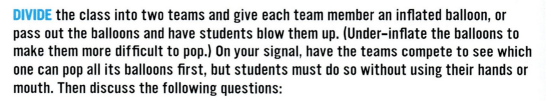

 JUMP-START THEIR HEARTS
TIME: 5–10 minutes

OPTION 1: BREAKING POINT
MATERIALS NEEDED: An inflated balloon for each student

DIVIDE the class into two teams and give each team member an inflated balloon, or pass out the balloons and have students blow them up. (Under-inflate the balloons to make them more difficult to pop.) On your signal, have the teams compete to see which one can pop all its balloons first, but students must do so without using their hands or mouth. Then discuss the following questions:

- **What caused the balloons to burst?** (Pressure was applied until they reached a breaking point.)
- **What causes people to sometimes reach a "breaking point" in their ability to withstand pressure, either from problems or from other people pressuring them to do things?**

ASK students what would have made the balloons pop more easily. Someone will likely point out that if the balloons were blown up more—with more pressure inside—they would tend to break more easily. Then blow up a balloon, but don't tie it.

POINT OUT that the more pressure and stress we allow ourselves to hold on the inside, the more vulnerable we are to "popping" unexpectedly. **But when we turn to God for help and allow His peace to relieve some of our pressure and stress** (slowly let air out of the balloon), **we become much more flexible and better able to hold up under pressure. Spending time with God allows Him to empty us of the world's pressure, so we never reach a breaking point.**

OPTION 2: DOMINO EFFECT
MATERIALS NEEDED: Two sets of dominoes (the more in each set, the better)

DIVIDE the class into two teams, and give each team a set of dominoes. Allow no more than five minutes to see which team can set up the most creative configuration that will fall in a chain reaction when the first domino is toppled. (They can use tables, chairs, books, or anything in the room.) When students are finished, have them test their "domino effect." Then discuss the following question:

- **How are people sometimes like these dominoes?** (People tend to follow other people. When one person does something, others often imitate it, even if it causes them to "fall.")

EXPLAIN that when a friend—even a Christian—falls because of peer pressure, others often fall as well. But we don't have to be a victim of the domino effect. **It's been said that "No one sins alone." In short, when you fall, you will likely pull others down with you. Does anyone have an example of this?**

SET UP a row of standing dominoes in front of you on a table or podium—as if you are going to knock them down.

ASK students what would happen if you took one or two dominoes out of the line. (Remove a couple consecutive dominoes, so that when you push the first one down, the gap from the missing pieces stops the rest from falling.)

- **What effect can we have on others if we refuse to give in to pressure to do things we know are not right or best?** (We can be the ones to stop the domino effect and can keep others from falling. In the process, we can inspire others to resist pressure and to stand up for what's right.)

INSTANT REPLAY

TIME: 5 minutes

MATERIALS NEEDED: Student Field Manual or "Instant Replay Discussion Guide" (Reproducible 3.1 from D2BDTeacher.com)

DIVIDE the class into pairs or threes. Refer to last session's "Daniel Dare" on pages 30–31 of the student Field Manual and/or distribute copies of the "Instant Replay Discussion Guide" for session 3. Have students share with their partners how their personal time with God went since the last session. (They don't have to tell how much time they set aside, but perhaps when and where they chose to spend it.) Use the following questions to guide the discussion:

- **Did you find it easy or difficult to stick to the discipline of daily time in the Word and prayer?**
- **What helped you stick to your commitment, and what kinds of distractions made it difficult?**
- **What's one thing God taught you or began to show you during your time with Him?**

 THE REEL WORLD, CLIP 3, THE ONE WITH THE CELLPHONE PICTURE

TIME: 5 minutes

MATERIALS NEEDED: DVD // "Reel World Discussion Guide" (Reproducible 3.2 from D2BDTeacher.com)

PLAY *The Reel World*, clip 3, "Dare to Be Discerning." Grant has invited his new friend Jason to join a group of their peers hanging out at the rec center. The innocent tide quickly turns when all the friends start looking at something inappropriate on Asa's cellphone. They call out for Grant and Jason to join them. Jason has no clue about these friends; he's watching Grant to see how to respond.

After the video, discuss the following questions using the "Reel World Discussion Guide" for clip 3:

- **Would you look at it? What if they offer to forward it to you as a friend? What would you say to this group? To Jason?**
- **What do we know about Grant's friends now? What do you think Jason thinks about all this?**
- **Why does it matter so much who we hang out with?**

 HERE WE GO
TIME: 20–25 minutes (including the main Bible reading)

MATERIALS NEEDED: "Xtreme Truth" Bible script list from pages 38–39 of the student Field Manual (or Reproducible 3.3 from **D2BDTeacher.com**) // Assorted items for the cast of characters listed on pages 63–64 // Jewelry item with a diamond, or photo of a diamond // Board and chalk or markers

IMPORTANT LEADER NOTE: Unless you have an extended time period, you will *not* be able to cover all of the material in this main teaching session. The segmented format with blue directives allows you to pick and choose the paragraphs, portions, questions, illustrations, etc., that are best suited to your class and time frame. The material here is not intended to be used word for word, but simply to provide direction so you can convey the content in your own style.

- What do you think of when you hear the term "peer pressure"?

- Why do people often do something—including what they know isn't right—just because others are doing it? (They want to fit in or impress others. They don't want to seem odd or afraid to do what others are willing to do.)

DISCUSS the term "peer pressure," which usually has to do with feeling pressed to do things we know are not best—or right. People who give in to negative peer pressure often do so because they've allowed themselves to be surrounded by bad influences.

POINT OUT that peer pressure is easier to resist when we have friends who are determined to do what's right and who are devoted to following God. If we choose friends who encourage wise choices, then positive peer pressure can inspire us to be stronger in our faith and to do great things for God.

THIS SESSION highlights the experience of Daniel's friends Shadrach, Meshach, and Abednego, whose devotion to God was tested to the extreme. Together, they refused to compromise their faith. With their lives on the line, they entrusted themselves to God, refusing to cave in to the pressures around them. As a result, they had the kind of impact on their world that many of us only dream about.

Daniel 3 : 1-30

1 King Nebuchadnezzar made an image of gold, whose height was sixty cubits and its breadth six cubits. He set it up on the plain of Dura, in the province of Babylon. 2 Then King Nebuchadnezzar sent to gather the satraps, the prefects, and the governors, the counselors, the treasurers, the justices, the magistrates, and all the officials of the provinces to come to the dedication of the image that King Nebuchadnezzar had set up. 3 Then the satraps, the prefects, and the governors, the counselors, the treasurers, the justices, the magistrates, and all the officials of the provinces gathered for the dedication of the image that King Nebuchadnezzar had set up. And they stood before the image that Nebuchadnezzar had set up. 4 And the herald proclaimed aloud, "You are commanded, O peoples, nations, and languages, 5 that when you hear the sound of the horn, pipe, lyre, trigon, harp, bagpipe, and every kind of music, you are to fall down and worship the golden image that King Nebuchadnezzar has set up. 6 And whoever does not fall down and worship shall immediately be cast into a burning fiery furnace."
7 Therefore, as soon as all the peoples heard the sound of the horn, pipe, lyre, trigon, harp, bagpipe, and every kind of music, all the peoples, nations, and languages fell down and worshiped the golden image that King Nebuchadnezzar had set up.

8 Therefore at that time certain Chaldeans came forward and maliciously accused the Jews. 9 They declared to King Nebuchadnezzar, "O king, live forever! 10 You, O king, have made a decree, that every man who hears the sound of the horn, pipe, lyre, trigon, harp, bagpipe, and every kind of music, shall fall down and worship the golden image. 11 And whoever does not fall down and worship shall be cast into a burning fiery furnace. 12 There are certain Jews whom you have appointed over the affairs of the province of Babylon: Shadrach, Meshach, and Abednego. These men, O king, pay no attention to you; they do not serve your gods or worship the golden image that you have set up."

13 Then Nebuchadnezzar in furious rage commanded that Shadrach, Meshach, and Abednego be brought. So they brought these men before the king. 14 Nebuchadnezzar answered and said to them, "Is it true, O Shadrach, Meshach, and Abednego, that you do not serve my gods or worship the golden image that I have set up? 15 Now if you are ready when you hear the sound of the horn, pipe, lyre, trigon, harp, bagpipe, and every kind of music, to fall down and worship the image that I have made, well and good. But if you do not worship, you shall immediately be cast into a burning fiery furnace. And who is the god who will deliver you out of my hands?"

16 Shadrach, Meshach, and Abednego answered and said to the king, "O Nebuchadnezzar, we have no need to answer you in this matter. **17** If this be so, our God whom we serve is able to deliver us from the burning fiery furnace, and he will deliver us out of your hand, O king. **18** But if not, be it known to you, O king, that we will not serve your gods or worship the golden image that you have set up."

19 Then Nebuchadnezzar was filled with fury, and the expression of his face was changed against Shadrach, Meshach, and Abednego. He ordered the furnace heated seven times more than it was usually heated. **20** And he ordered some of the mighty men of his army to bind Shadrach, Meshach, and Abednego, and to cast them into the burning fiery furnace. **21** Then these men were bound in their cloaks, their tunics, their hats, and their other garments, and they were thrown into the burning fiery furnace. **22** Because the king's order was urgent and the furnace overheated, the flame of the fire killed those men who took up Shadrach, Meshach, and Abednego. **23** And these three men, Shadrach, Meshach, and Abednego, fell bound into the burning fiery furnace.

24 Then King Nebuchadnezzar was astonished and rose up in haste. He declared to his counselors, "Did we not cast three men bound into the fire?" They answered and said to the king, "True, O king." **25** He answered and said, "But I see four men unbound, walking in the midst of the fire, and they are not hurt; and the appearance of the fourth is like a son of the gods."

26 Then Nebuchadnezzar came near to the door of the burning fiery furnace; he declared, "Shadrach, Meshach, and Abednego, servants of the Most High God, come out, and come here!" Then Shadrach, Meshach, and Abednego came out from the fire. **27** And the satraps, the prefects, the governors, and the king's counselors gathered together and saw that the fire had not had any power over the bodies of those men. The hair of their heads was not singed, their cloaks were not harmed, and no smell of fire had come upon them.
28 Nebuchadnezzar answered and said, "Blessed be the God of Shadrach, Meshach, and Abednego, who has sent his angel and delivered his servants, who trusted in him, and set aside the king's command, and yielded up their bodies rather than serve and worship any god except their own God. **29** Therefore I make a decree: Any people, nation, or language that speaks anything against the God of Shadrach, Meshach, and Abednego shall be torn limb from limb, and their houses laid in ruins, for there is no other god who is able to rescue in this way." **30** Then the king promoted Shadrach, Meshach, and Abednego in the province of Babylon.

BEFORE reading Daniel chapter 3, recruit volunteers to act out the parts described below. (If your group is small, have individuals act out parts that call for several people, or have people play multiple parts.) Give each volunteer a copy of the "Xtreme Truth" Bible script (Reproducible 3.3 from **D2BDTeacher.com**). This script is also on pages 38–39 of the student Field Manual.

PROVIDE the characters with the props described below and tell them to quickly acquaint themselves with their parts.

(LEADER NOTE: Unless you have a longer class period, you will *not* have time to distribute and use the props [otherwise it might take you 15 minutes just to cover the Bible passage]. Without props, the actors can simply pretend to have the things described [cellphones, etc.].)

- **KING NEBUCHADNEZZAR**
  Carries a stick, pole, microphone stand, or something that can pass for a royal scepter; also wears a cape, old suit coat, or jacket, as if it's a royal robe.

- **GOLDEN IMAGE**
  Lies stiff on the ground and stays stiff as the kings sets him or her upright; can also wear a bucket or pail on the head.

- **ALL GOVERNMENT OFFICIALS** (satraps, prefects, governors, etc.)
  Several kids who carry assorted office implements or devices like cellphones, PDAs, laptops; look as "official" as possible.

- **THE HERALD** (to announce the king's proclamation about the gold image)
  Carries a megaphone or cheerleading cone (which could be made from a large, rolled-up sheet of paper).

- **GROUP OF PEOPLE** (who worship the image)
  Keep bowing in the direction of the image and kneel down in front of it when "music" plays.

- **ASTROLOGERS**
  Keep looking up, shake their fingers at the young men who don't bow to image, tattle on the youths to the king.

- **SHADRACH, MESHACH, AND ABEDNEGO**
  Three normal-looking kids or teens who turn their back on the image; not too disrespectful, but continue to talk casually among themselves.

- **BLAZING FURNACE**
  Several kids who stand in a semicircle, waving arms and swaying like flames.

- **SOLDIERS** (to bind the young men and throw them into fire)
  Two kids with helmets, who stand tall.

(**LEADER NOTE:** Inform the characters that because you want to read the entire chapter in a timely fashion, they'll have to act it out at "full speed." In other words, read at a normal pace and let the actors keep up. The added commotion will provide humor.)

In Daniel chapter 3, King Nebuchadnezzar pridefully sets up a statue in his own honor. He was likely trying to use a form of religion to unite all the territories he recently added to his empire. Demanding worship toward the image was a way of promoting loyalty to himself. During the dedication ceremony, a proclamation commanded that whenever the people heard the music, they were to bow to the image. Those who refused would be executed.

- **Why wouldn't the three young men bow to the king's image?** (It didn't matter what everyone else was doing; their loyalty was to God, and they trusted Him to take care of them.)

- **Looking at Daniel 3:16–18, does anything surprise you about the young men's response to the king? If so, what?** (They didn't need to reconsider their decision, nor did they try to defend themselves. They knew that God could rescue them from anything the king had in store. Even if God didn't spare them from the fire, they wouldn't deny Him.)

POINT OUT that enduring tough times and influencing others for Christ starts with a firm commitment to honor God.

- **How do you think these young men found the strength to stand so boldly for what they believed?** (As we've already seen, Daniel and his friends were deeply devoted to God. Because of this, God helped them develop the character qualities and personality traits that kept them firmly committed to His standards of right and wrong. That has to do with character.)

EXPLAIN that enduring tough times and influencing others for Christ requires—and builds—godly character. **By relying on God and practicing things we learn from Him through prayer and His Word, we develop the wisdom, strength, desire, and discipline to stand strong under pressure.**

- **How can your character affect your influence for Jesus?** (How you live and the standards to which you hold yourself can either add to or take away from your witness. If your attitudes, conversations, and behavior aren't good, then people may get the wrong impression of Jesus, and they probably won't listen when you talk about Him. If you behave more like Jesus, however, people are more likely to listen. Godly character gives credibility to your witness.)

EMPHASIZE that we also need to be that godly friend who encourages and supports others. Challenge students to consider someone they can influence by being a good, godly friend.

- **How do you think the friendship between Shadrach, Meshach, and Abednego helped them in this situation?**

ILLUSTRATION: Display a diamond or photo of a diamond (or draw a representation of one on the board). Ask students if they know how these gems are formed. Explain that diamonds basically consist of the element carbon. At one point they are coal. But over many years, intense geologic pressure deep below the earth's surface can transform a worthless lump of coal into a beautiful and treasured jewel. Just as some forms of pressure are useful in nature, we can benefit from positive peer pressure.

- **In what way can friends—particularly Christians—exert positive peer pressure?** (They can encourage us to do what's right—to keep serving God and obeying His Word. They can also inspire us to talk about and demonstrate our faith in ways that can influence others for God.)

EMPHASIZE how godly friends can help us endure tough times and influence others for Jesus.

- **The title of this session is "Dare to Be Discerning." What does it mean to have discernment?** (It means showing good judgment and making wise and appropriate choices.)

- **How does having discernment apply to friendships?** (We should choose friends wisely, because who we hang around with influences what we do and affects our character.)

Proverbs 13:20 says, *"Whoever walks with the wise becomes wise, but the companion of fools will suffer harm."*

Proverbs 27:17 says, *"Iron sharpens iron, and one man sharpens another."*

- **What does it mean for people to "sharpen" each other, and how can godly friends do this?** (Friends with good character can challenge, encourage, and inspire us to be better and to accomplish more. Friends who follow Jesus can keep us from feeling that we're serving Him by ourselves.)

EXPLAIN that it takes discernment to recognize idols that our culture tries to get us to bow down to. **These false "gods" may not be as obvious as a big gold statue, but they can distract and deceive us just the same. To resist bad influences, it helps to have friends who encourage us to do what's right.**

- **What are some of the idols in our culture today that people tend to honor or worship?** (These could be people, things, or even activities. An idol is anything that gets more of our attention than it should, distracts our attention from God, or takes priority over Him.)

- **In what situations might Christians today be tested like Shadrach, Meshach, and Abednego?** (People might try to persuade us to participate in things we know aren't right. They might even reject or make fun of us because of our faith. But this is mild compared to what some people face. In many parts of the world, identifying with Jesus can still lead to imprisonment or death.)

EXPLAIN that following Jesus won't spare us from trouble. **In fact, Jesus told us to expect trouble and opposition** (see John 16:33). **Yet despite constant pressure to compromise our commitment to God, we must remember that if we're ashamed of Him now, He will be ashamed of us on Judgment Day** (Mark 8:38; Luke 9:26). **But if we boldly identify with Him, He will stand with us now and forever.**

Romans 1:16 says, *"For I am not ashamed of the gospel, for it is the power of God for salvation to everyone who believes, to the Jew first and also to the Greek."*

EXPLAIN that the *ability to endure tough times and influence others for Christ hinges on the choices we make.* **We must deliberately decide to do things that will help us be strong when facing difficulties and opposition. At the same time, we must avoid activities and behaviors that make it more difficult to live for God and withstand the pressures we'll face as we follow Jesus.**

- **In what ways can we prepare for persecution, and how can we gain the strength to stand for our faith in God?** (We can let people know where we stand from the start, so they don't expect us to compromise what we believe. As we considered in the last session, we also grow in our relationship with God by spending time daily in His Word and in prayer.)

EXPLAIN that when the king saw that the young men would not compromise, he was furious *"and the expression of his face was changed against* [*them*]" (Daniel 3:19). He ordered that the furnace be made seven times hotter than usual and commanded his strongest soldiers to bind Shadrach, Meshach, and Abednego and throw them into the fire. Then something supernatural happened.

- **Looking back at Daniel 3:24–30, what were some miraculous aspects of the young men's rescue from the fire?** (They had been tightly bound when thrown in but were freely walking and unharmed when the king saw them. Most amazing, there was a fourth person in the fire, who looked *"like a son of the gods"* [v. 25].)

EXPLAIN that when the king called the young men out of the fire, the royal officials were amazed that not a hair on their heads or fiber of their robes was singed. They didn't even smell like smoke. But the greatest miracle was the impact they had on others as a result of their unwavering devotion to God.

- **What influence did the young men's actions have?** (Not only did the king praise God, he made a decree that no one in his kingdom was to speak against God, because no other god had the power to save like this. By refusing to deny God, these young men influenced an entire nation.)

EXPLAIN that Shadrach, Meshach, and Abednego defied peer pressure and risked their lives to stay true to God—and God honored them for it. If you stay true to God, regardless of the consequences, He promises to be with you *"when you walk through fire"* (Isaiah 43:2), and He won't allow you to face more than you can handle with His help (1 Corinthians 10:13). Jesus said that even in the most extreme circumstances, we shouldn't worry about what to say, because the Holy Spirit will give us the words to witness for Him (Matthew 10:19–20).

As we considered in the last session, we represent Christ to a spiritually lost world.

2 Corinthians 5:18, 20 says, *"All this is from God, who through Christ reconciled us to himself and gave us the ministry of reconciliation … . Therefore, we are ambassadors for Christ, God making his appeal through us. We implore you on behalf of Christ, be reconciled to God."*

- **What does it mean to be reconciled to God and have the ministry of reconciliation?** (Jesus restored the opportunity for us to "get right" with God and have a relationship with Him. We're now instructed to let others know what He did for us and how He can do the same for them.)

- **What does it mean that we are Christ's ambassadors and God makes His appeal through us?** (Those who have a relationship with Jesus represent Him to others.)

CHALLENGE students to consider the impressions they give others of God. Discuss how words, attitudes, and actions can affect others' views of God and their openness to His message.

LIST on the board, in two columns, students' responses to these two questions:

- **What can we do to make the Christian life appealing?**

- **What can we do that would tend to make it unattractive?**

Consider the items in both categories and discuss whether or not we can go "too far" in order to make the Gospel appealing. Encourage students to explain their reasoning.

EXPLAIN that we'll never influence non-Christians to consider Christ if we only spend time with Christians. But we must be careful not to get into close relationships with people who pull us away from God.

- **How can we have non-Christian friends and be accepted by them without compromising our values and our ability to influence others to trust Jesus?**

EXPLAIN that we must never underestimate the impact we can have on others by boldly identifying with Christ and refusing to compromise our devotion to Him. **As we considered in the first session, Christ's followers must be different from their surrounding culture. Even people who don't follow Jesus expect Christians to live differently. People who want to effectively influence others for Christ may need to make some relationship and lifestyle changes.**

DISCUSS with students the kinds of changes they might need to make to effectively influence others for Jesus and give them a more accurate impression of what it means to follow Him.

HANGING BY A WIRE
TIME: 3 minutes

Would you drive over a bridge that was hanging by a wire? People do it every day as they cross one of the most recognizable structural landmarks in the country. San Francisco's Golden Gate Bridge was the longest in the world at the time of completion and still has the seventh-longest span. It crosses 1.7 miles, is 90 feet wide, weighs 887,000 tons, and hangs 220 feet above water by wires—lots of them.

The Golden Gate is suspended by two main cables that cross the tops of its two towers and are secured in concrete at each end. Each cable is over 36 inches in diameter and consists of 27,572 smaller wires. The two main cables contain enough wire to stretch 80,000 miles.*

By itself, no individual wire could suspend even one vehicle. Yet bound together, the wires support approximately 40 million car crossings per year and have held up for over 2 billion crossings since the bridge opened in 1937. That's the power of being bound together—a principle that applies even more to people than it does to wires.

Ecclesiastes 4:12

"And though a man might prevail against one who is alone, two will withstand him—a threefold cord is not quickly broken."

The power of positive friendships can enhance your life in so many ways, including your witness for Jesus. You don't need 27,572 friends. Just a few good ones can make all the difference.

*Source: gocalifornia.about.com

BIBLE IN YOUR BRAIN
TIME: 5–10 minutes

MATERIALS NEEDED: Bibles and/or pages 40–41 in the student Field Manual (or Reproducible 3.4 from **D2BDTeacher.com**)

INVITE students to look at what else the Bible says about taking a bold stand for God and about the effect that our relationships can have on our influence for Christ. (Have volunteers read the passages one at a time. Some of these you will recognize from the main teaching time. If you have time, briefly discuss the implications of each.)

(**LEADER NOTE:** Depending on your time frame, you may want to cover only a few of these passages, as students will cover most of them in brief devotional segments in their Field Manuals.)

Romans 1:16
"For I am not ashamed of the gospel, for it is the power of God for salvation to everyone who believes, to the Jew first and also to the Greek."

Proverbs 28:1, NLT
"The wicked run away when no one is chasing them, but the godly are as bold as lions."

1 Corinthians 15:33
"Do not be deceived: 'Bad company ruins good morals.'"

Proverbs 27:17
"Iron sharpens iron, and one man sharpens another."

Ecclesiastes 4:10, 12
"For if they fall, one will lift up his fellow. But woe to him who is alone when he falls and has not another to lift him up! ... And though a man might prevail against one who is alone, two will withstand him—a threefold cord is not quickly broken."

2 Corinthians 5:18, 20
"All this is from God, who through Christ reconciled us to himself and gave us the ministry of reconciliation ... . Therefore, we are ambassadors for Christ, God making his appeal through us. We implore you on behalf of Christ, be reconciled to God."

Proverbs 13:20
"Whoever walks with the wise becomes wise, but the companion of fools will suffer harm."

EXPLAIN that our relationships have a huge impact on who we are and what we do. Developing good, godly friendships makes it easier to boldly stand for God and influence others to follow Jesus.

REFER students to pages 40—41 of the Field Manual, where they will find these passages, along with a practical challenge and prayer focus for each day of the coming week.

ACTIVITY ZONE
TIME: 5—10 minutes (Optional, depending on the session time frame)

OPTION 1: CROWD CONTROL
MATERIALS NEEDED: "Crowd Control" survey (Reproducible 3.5 from D2BDTeacher.com) // Pens or pencils

DISTRIBUTE copies of Reproducible 3.5—"Crowd Control"—and pens or pencils. At the top of the sheet is a scale ranging from 1 (Completely False/Never) to 5 (Always/Completely True). Have students respond to each statement with a number, 1 through 5, depending on the frequency with which their friends do the following:

- Most of my friends share interests similar to mine.

- My friends make me feel good about myself.

- People I hang around with spend more time building people up than gossiping.

- My friends encourage me to listen to them rather than to my parents.
- My parents like my friends.
- When I am around my friends, I am a better person.
- I feel like my friends really know what I am all about.
- I can talk to my friends freely about my relationship with God.
- My friends give me good advice that fits with God's Word rather than worldly "wisdom."
- My friends inspire me to serve God rather than follow my own interests.
- My friends are a good influence on my life.
- My friends join with me in trying to influence others for Jesus.

CHALLENGE students to consider their responses and then to consider the quality of their friendships. Are their best friends drawing them closer to, or away from, God's plan for their lives?

DISCUSS with students how their friendships can affect their behavior in positive and negative ways.

- **How can we maintain the balance between having friends that inspire us to live for Christ and having friends who don't know Jesus and whom we can influence for Him?**

OPTION 2: TUG OF WAR
MATERIALS NEEDED: Long rope with strip of cloth tied at the middle // Taped line marking the middle of the floor

DIVIDE the group into two teams of relatively equal size and strength (being careful not to offend anyone about their size or strength in the process). Have the teams get in line on opposite ends of a long rope for an old-fashioned tug of war. Tie a strip of cloth at the middle of the rope, and mark a midpoint line on the floor to align with the middle of the rope to start the game.

GIVE the teams a minute or two to adjust their positions on the rope and determine strategy. Have both teams pull on the rope enough to get it lined up in the middle. On your signal, each team will try to pull the opposite team completely across the middle line. The first to do so wins. (Be careful not to let anyone get hurt or knock anything over.) Then discuss the following:

ASK students if, as Christians, they ever feel like they're getting pulled from two different directions—one bringing you closer to Jesus and the other taking you away from Him.

- **What kinds of influences tend to pull us closer to God and help us accomplish His plans?**

- **What kinds of influences tend to pull us away from God and His plans?**

- **What strategies can help a team in a game of tug of war?** (It helps to get good footing, hold on to something, pull at the right time, or just be stronger to begin with.)

- **How could these strategies apply in a spiritual sense to your relationship with Jesus and your ability to "pull" others closer to Him? In other words, how can you get better footing or gain momentum spiritually?** (Spending time in prayer and God's Word gives us a solid base, and applying what God teaches us provides strength and momentum to live for God more effectively.)

EXPLAIN that if we're going to be effective at bringing people to Jesus, rather than letting them pull us away from Him, we must be on solid spiritual footing, constantly growing stronger in our relationship with Him. Once we gain spiritual momentum, we need to keep moving and putting into practice what God teaches through times in prayer, Bible reading, worship, and ministry.

WITNESS WORK
TIME: 10 minutes

MATERIALS NEEDED: Student Field Manual (or Reproducible 3.6, "Conversational Connections," from **D2BDTeacher.com**) // Board and chalk or markers // "Steps to Peace With God" witnessing tool

EXPLAIN that the most effective way to influence people for Jesus is through personal relationships. **One of the keys to building relationships is finding common ground— something others can relate to. It's unlikely that anyone will come up to you and say, "How can I be saved?" If your life is noticeably different, however, they might ask you about it. If you learn how to turn everyday conversations into spiritual ones, you'll have opportunities to talk about Jesus.**

ASK students to name topics they frequently talk about with others, and list responses on the board. If they have trouble coming up with topics, you might suggest these: sports, family, friends, popularity, music, movies, clothes, games, weekends, the opposite sex, authority figures, technology, etc.

EXPLAIN that an "open door" can turn a typical conversation into an opportunity to talk about God or spiritual issues. For example, in John chapter 4, Jesus began talking to the woman at the well about water. But the conversation moved to another level when He said, "Whoever drinks the water I give will never thirst." Open doors can be questions, comments, ideas, or personal examples.

REFER to the list of topics students suggested. Brainstorm ways to turn conversations about these issues into discussions about spiritual things.

POINT OUT that making a conversational transition won't always lead to conversations about Jesus. But the goal is eventually to get the opportunity to share your personal experience so others might consider Christ for themselves.

REFER students to "Conversational Connections" section on page 42 in their Field Manuals. If they don't have manuals, use Reproducible 3.6, "Conversational Connections," from **D2BDTeacher.com**. Between now and the next session, students will list a few more of their own ideas for conversation starters and transitions.

HIGHLIGHT Step 3 of the "Steps to Peace With God" witnessing tool, along with the related Bible verses that they'll memorize between now and the next session.

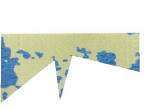

THE OWN-ZONE
TIME: 5 minutes

MATERIALS NEEDED: Blank paper or "Own-Zone Response Sheet" (Reproducible 3.7 from D2BDTeacher.com) // Pens or pencils

DISTRIBUTE paper (or copies of Reproducible 3.7) and pens or pencils. Allow each student to find a place where he or she can get alone with God and write and pray privately. Have students divide their sheets into three sections. Then have them label and fill in their sheets as follows:

1. **Top section: "Potential Idols"**—Write two or three things that could become "idols" in your life if you're not careful. This includes anything or anyone that detracts attention from God or takes priority over His purposes.

2. **Middle section: "Relationships and Lifestyle"**—Briefly describe a couple aspects of your life that may need to change in order for you to have the positive influence He intends for you to have on others. This could involve a relationship you need to change, get out of, or develop. It could also be an attitude, activity, or behavior that's questionable or that you know is not right.

3. **Bottom section: "Positive Peers"**—List several Christian acquaintances along with any Christian peers with whom you could develop a friendship. These are people you can encourage and with whom you could partner to have more effective influence for Jesus.

GIVE students time to reflect on what they've written and to use their sheets as prayer guides. Encourage them to rely on God for strength and discipline to rid their lives of potential idols, rearrange their priorities, and make the lifestyle changes necessary to fit God's purposes for their lives.

ENCOURAGE students to pray for their Christian peers daily, asking God to help them have a positive effect on each other's lives and to inspire boldness in their Christian witness.

CHALLENGE students to keep these sheets in their Bibles or Field Manuals and to continue using them as prayer guides in the days ahead. Encourage them to connect with the Christian peers they listed, planning a time to get together to talk about ways they can work together to reach others for Jesus.

THE DANIEL DARE

TIME: 5–10 minutes

MATERIALS NEEDED: Student Field Manual
(or Reproducible 3.8, "Daniel Dare" for session 3, from
D2BDTeacher.com)

REFER students to pages 48–49 in the Field Manual. (If they don't have manuals, distribute copies of Reproducible 3.8.) If you have extended time, students can start on this exercise now; otherwise, briefly describe what they'll do outside of class.

EXPLAIN that at the end of the lesson we considered how having more effective influence for Jesus may require some relationship and lifestyle changes. That's because who we are and how we act can speak louder than what we say. **Effectively influencing others to trust Christ takes more than having the guts to tell people about Jesus. It means that how we think and act needs to be consistent with what we say. This doesn't mean we have to be perfect. But our friendship with Jesus should be getting stronger and more consistent so that we give a good impression of what it means to follow Jesus.**

PROVIDE a few minutes for students to list in their manuals some of the things that they intend to start doing (or do more often) and the things they intend to stop doing. Then in the space provided, also have them list some individuals they need to:

- Hang out with more (because they are a good influence and inspire faith)
- Hang out with less—or not at all (because they are a negative influence)
- Spend time with so they can influence them for Jesus

CHALLENGE students to come back next week prepared to share what they experienced as they followed through on this "Daniel Dare."

CLOSING
TIME: 5 minutes

REMIND students that *the ability to endure tough challenges and influence others for Christ hinges on their commitment, character, companionships, and choices.* In order for their witness to be credible—or believable—they must rely on God and put His Word into practice so they become more like Jesus. That way, others can get a more accurate impression of what He's like and what it means to follow Him. A vital part of their influence has to do with relationships and lifestyle. In order to effectively fulfill God's purpose, they may need to make some changes in these areas.

ENCOURAGE students to continue praying for the three people they listed last week that they hope to lead to Christ. Give them a couple minutes to do so right now.

ASK for a volunteer or two to close in prayer, or lead students in the following prayer:

Dear Jesus, thank You for always being with me and for helping me fulfill Your purposes for my life through both good and bad times. Teach me to become more like You so that others get a good impression of what You're like and what You can do in their lives. Give me a boldness and determination to stand up for Your truth and to resist bowing down to the world's idols. Help me to build relationships with people who will challenge me to be a more effective witness for You, and help me to be that kind of friend to others as well. I ask this in Your Name, Jesus. Amen.

DON'T FORGET the memory work, daily devotions, and "Daniel Dare" in the student Field Manual. Be prepared to share your progress in the next session.

Dare to Be His Disciple

Key Focus: We can point others to Christ by following His example of self-sacrifice and humble service.

SESSION OVERVIEW

We often tell kids to follow their dreams, assuming that this will bring out their full potential and take them down a path of fulfillment. While such advice is well-intended, it can actually deprive kids of the life they were meant to lead. Only when our goals line up with God's goals can we experience the ultimate peace, joy, and satisfaction God intends. For a Christian, life is not simply about following dreams; it's about following Jesus Christ and fulfilling God's purpose. In the process, a follower of Christ will experience fulfillment beyond human imagination. This doesn't mean that everything in life will be easy or convenient. In fact, God's purposes typically take us down unexpected paths. Yet, nothing else satisfies like living for Jesus and patterning our lives after His example.

In this session, you'll challenge students to be lifelong learners and followers of Christ, with faith that's evident in their actions and focused on leading others into a personal relationship with God. This will require sacrifice and readiness to serve the needs of others, many of whom will never receive the message of Jesus unless it comes from someone with uncompromising character and undeniable compassion. By considering Daniel's behavior in the face of life-threatening opposition, students will see how godly boldness and selfless humility can work together to powerfully point people to Christ.

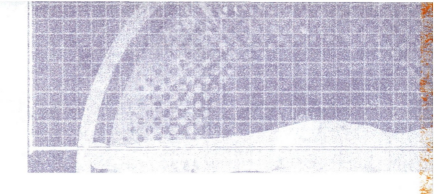

Through this session, students will learn:

- To consider the extraordinary impact of ordinary people who follow God's way instead of their own.
- To realize how their actions can speak louder than their words.
- How following Jesus' example of humble service provides opportunities to influence others for Him.
- To examine their behavior and identify what needs to change to strengthen their witness for Christ.
- To realize that as they obey God in every aspect of life—public and private—they will have opportunities to share their faith.

PLANNING & PREP

For this session, you'll need:

1. Student Field Manuals (one per student)
2. Bibles (one per student)
3. Paper and pens/pencils for all students
4. Reproducibles for Lesson 4 from **D2BDTeacher.com**
5. *The Reel World* DVD (clip 4)
6. Glass of water with ice // Thick string // Salt
7. Board and chalk or markers
8. "Steps to Peace With God" witnessing tool (one per student)

 JUMP-START THEIR HEARTS
TIME: 5–10 minutes

OPTION 1: CLASS ACT
MATERIALS NEEDED: "Class Act" (Reproducible 4.1 from D2BDTeacher.com)

BEFORE THE SESSION: Cut apart the phrase cards from Reproducible 4.1, "Class Act," or come up with your own phrases and write them on 14 individual notecards.

DIVIDE the class into two groups of equal size and separate the teams on either side of the room. (If you have at least five of each gender, you could pit guys against girls for a spirited competition.) Provide each team with a stack of seven cards with the phrases facedown on the floor.

THE CONTEST is an old-fashioned, action-packed game of charades in which participants will act out phrases without speaking, only using actions and gestures. Facial expressions are acceptable, but the actors cannot mouth the words as they try to get their teammates to guess the phrases they're acting out. Actors can nod or point to people who guess parts of a phrase to confirm that they are on the right track. (You might allow one person from each team to monitor the other team's actors to ensure that everyone follows the rules.)

ON YOUR SIGNAL, the first person on each team will come to the front and take the card from the top of his or her team's stack. (He or she should look at that card only and not show it to anyone else.) That person must proceed to act out the phrase according to the rules given above. When a team member guesses the entire phrase correctly, he or she must rush to the front, look at the next phrase, and proceed to act it out. Each team can skip two phrases if the team can't guess them. This is a race, so the first team to guess five phrases correctly wins.

EXPLAIN that when it comes to sharing our faith and reaching people for Christ, our actions often speak louder than our words. Though we must actually tell people about Jesus, if our attitudes and behavior aren't consistent with His character and message, then people are not likely to listen or believe.

(See ILLUSTRATION after Option 2.)

OPTION 2: RECOGNIZING JESUS
MATERIALS NEEDED: None

BEFORE THE SESSION: Search various sources from literature, print media, and the Internet to find artists' depictions of Jesus. Find ones that don't look typical. Display the images one by one, starting with the least obvious. Ask students whom this represents. After they "recognize" Jesus, ask them to describe how they think the artists got their ideas of what He looked like. Then discuss the following questions:

- **What do you think Jesus looked like while on earth? Where do you get your perceptions of His appearance?** (Many get this from a picture or movie.)

- **What do you think Jesus looks like now? Do you think He shows Himself literally to people today? Why or why not? If so, how?**

- **Do you think you would recognize Jesus if you met Him? Why or why not?**

EXPLAIN that regardless of our perception of Jesus in this life, one day we will all meet Him face to face. On that day, there will be no mistaking who Jesus is. But unless people get to know Him personally before that time, it will be too late. So people need to see Jesus before then. But how?

- **How can people who don't have a personal relationship with Jesus get an idea of what He's like? How can we help them see what He's like?** (We must learn to become more like Jesus and live in a way that reflects Jesus' character so others can get a more accurate impression of what He's like.)

EXPLAIN that a big part of being like Jesus is demonstrating God's love—not just a feeling of concern, but active compassion that meets real needs. **Today we'll consider how we can reach out to others in a way that doesn't just tell people what Jesus is like, but actually shows them.**

ILLUSTRATION: Have you ever been in a grocery store and seen a lady handing out free samples of food? If you were hungry, would it fill you up? Probably not. But you might buy a whole package of that food. The samples are meant to whet your appetite so you'll buy the whole box. That's how it is with Jesus. Our lives should be like a sample of God's goodness. We don't just tell people about Jesus; we allow them to experience Christ through us. Our attitudes and actions can help people gain an appetite for Jesus.

85

🔥 INSTANT REPLAY

TIME: 5 minutes

MATERIALS NEEDED: Student Field Manual or "Instant Replay Discussion Guide" (Reproducible 4.2 from D2BDTeacher.com)

DIVIDE the class into pairs or threes. Refer to last session's "Daniel Dare" on pages 48–49 of the student Field Manual and/or distribute copies of the "Instant Replay Discussion Guide" for session 4. Have students briefly share with their partners if and how they followed through on the things they intended to start and stop doing. (They don't have to get specific on what they wanted to stop doing if these things are more personal.) Encourage each student to answer the following questions:

- **For those of you who made the effort to spend more time with the Lord, did you notice a difference in how you felt, what you experienced, or what happened to you this past week?** (Allow students to share their experiences.)

- **Who did you commit to spending more time with, and why?** (Have them tell about the Christians they wanted to be around more and the non-Christians they hoped to influence for Christ.)

🔥 THE REEL WORLD, CLIP 4, THE ONE ABOUT THE CONCERT

TIME: 5 minutes

MATERIALS NEEDED: DVD // "Reel World Discussion Guide" (Reproducible 4.3 from D2BDTeacher.com)

PLAY *The Reel World*, clip 4, "Dare to Be His Disciple." Chris and Asa have scored tickets to a concert they've been wanting to go to for some time. Problem: They find out it's the same weekend as VBS, which Asa already committed to help out with. What's a disciple of Christ to do? They're both "good" things ...

After the video, discuss the following questions using the "Reel World Discussion Guide" for clip 4:

- **What would you do? Both are good things, right?**
- **Which commitment is right to honor? Why?**
- **Is it really that big of a deal? What would each decision communicate to his friends? His church? God?**
- **As a disciple of Christ, what do you think would be the best choice?**

HERE WE GO

TIME: 20–25 minutes (including the main Bible reading)

MATERIALS NEEDED: Glass of water with ice // Thick string // Salt // Student Field Manual

IMPORTANT LEADER NOTE: Unless you have an extended time period, you will *not* be able to cover all of the material in this main teaching session. The segmented format with blue directives allows you to pick and choose the paragraphs, portions, questions, illustrations, etc., that are best suited to your class and time frame. The material here is not intended to be used word for word, but simply to provide direction so you can convey the content in your own style.

Over the past few sessions we've considered how serving God in an ungodly society will test our faith. We've seen how Daniel and his friends dared to be different, obeying God and refusing to compromise their devotion to Him. As a result, they had an extraordinary impact on their world.

- **If Daniel and his friends were here today, how do you think they would challenge you regarding your current lifestyle and your witness for Christ?**

- **Do you think God could use you as He did Daniel and his friends? Why or why not?**

EXPLAIN that many of us may not feel as bold or influential as Daniel and his friends. Yet, we must realize that Jesus can use ordinary people who are willing to put themselves aside and identify with Jesus. **Consider the type of individuals Jesus first called to follow Him.**

Matthew 4:18-20 says, *"While walking by the Sea of Galilee, he saw two brothers, Simon (who is called Peter) and Andrew his brother, casting a net into the sea, for they were fishermen. And he said to them, 'Follow me, and I will make you fishers of men.' Immediately they left their nets and followed him."*

- **What do you notice about the fishermen's response to Jesus?** (They left their own things and followed Jesus without hesitation.)

- **What do you think it means that Jesus would make them "*fishers of men*"?** (Speaking in terms that were relevant to Peter and Andrew, Jesus calls them to a higher mission than they've ever known—to influence others for God and introduce them to Christ.)

EXPLAIN that by the time Jesus returned to heaven, His influence—along with the power of the Holy Spirit—was evident in His disciples' lives. **When Peter and John were arrested for preaching about Jesus and were questioned by the religious rulers, they responded with boldness:**

"'And there is salvation in no one else, for there is no other name under heaven given among men by which we must be saved.' Now when they saw the boldness of Peter and John, and perceived that they were uneducated, common men, they were astonished. And they recognized that they had been with Jesus" **(Acts 4:12–13).**

EXPLAIN that we can be just as bold as Jesus' first disciples as we get to know Jesus and rely on the guidance of the Holy Spirit. Those who follow God's ways rather than their own can have extraordinary influence on others. That's part of what it means to be a disciple of Jesus.

- **What do you think it means to be Jesus' disciple?** (A disciple is a "disciplined follower" and a "learner." In session 2 we considered ways we can exercise discipline in our relationship with Jesus. By spending time in prayer and God's Word—then obeying what He teaches us—we can get to know Jesus and His plans for us so we can follow them effectively.)

EXPLAIN that doing these things takes discipline, which means putting aside some things for the sake of more important things. **Jesus said that following Him requires that kind of sacrifice.** *"Whoever does not bear his own cross and come after me cannot be my disciple"* **(Luke 14:27).**

- **What do you think it means to carry your cross?** (While the cross has become a popular icon, used for a variety of reasons, it's actually a brutal symbol of the pain and humiliation Jesus endured for a world that continually rejects Him. Yet no one will ever love us more. So regardless of what anyone thinks, we should boldly identify with Jesus, regardless of the difficulty that may bring.)

EXPLAIN that being Jesus' disciple involves identifying with Jesus and following His example. **This has a lot to do with what He told His disciples in Mark 10:42–45 about the true measure of greatness:**

"And Jesus called them to him and said to them, 'You know that those who are considered rulers of the Gentiles lord it over them, and their great ones exercise authority over them. But it shall not be so among you. But whoever would be great among you must be your servant, and whoever would be first among you must be slave of all. For even the Son of Man came not to be served but to serve, and to give his life as a ransom for many.'"

EXPLAIN that Jesus had influence and accomplished His mission because He was willing to serve. **By serving others and showing simple acts of kindness, you too can gain influence.**

- **How can serving others give you influence and affect your witness for Christ?** (By serving people, we model Christ's character and give them a more accurate impression of Jesus. Serving gives our faith credibility—it makes it more authentic and believable—and it can break down barriers of resistance to Jesus' life-changing message.)

- **In what practical ways do you think Jesus wants you to serve others?** (Encourage students to share examples of how they can serve at home, school, church, and in their community. At home they could help a family member with chores, clean the car, do the dishes without being asked, etc. At school they could carry someone's books or band instrument, share their favorite

dessert at lunch, or help a teacher tidy up a classroom. Wherever they are and whatever they're doing, they can show kindness and respect.)

EXPLAIN that some people will never listen to the message of Jesus unless it comes from someone who cares enough to meet their needs. In other words, we may have to feed people's stomachs before feeding their souls, or clean up their neighborhood before we can help clean up their lives. We can often do more to point people to Christ by serving them than by anything we say.

Looking at Daniel's example, we see several times when he honored God by serving others:

- In chapter 2, he relied on God's help to interpret King Nebuchadnezzar's dream when none of the king's psychics or counselors could. Daniel gave credit to God, and the king promoted Daniel to rule over the entire province of Babylon.

- In chapter 4, Daniel once again interpreted a dream. Though it wasn't favorable to the king, it did come true. Later, the king repented and honored God as Daniel had advised him to do.

- In chapter 5, Daniel served under another king, Belshazzar, who hosted a banquet in honor of Babylon's false gods, using items stolen from God's temple. Suddenly, what appeared to be a hand began to write on the wall. The terrified king offered gifts to anyone who could interpret the writing, but no one could. The king's wife suggested that he call on Daniel. With God's help, Daniel read the writing, predicting that the Medes and Persians would overrun Babylon. That night, the king was killed as Darius the Mede took over the empire.

- In chapter 6, Daniel served under Darius as one of three top leaders in the Persian Empire.

How could Daniel have such powerful influence, even though his faith in the true God was at odds with Babylonian culture? (Though Daniel didn't conform to the Babylonians' beliefs and lifestyles, he still served graciously and spoke God's truth whenever he had the opportunity. As a result, he was able to enlighten others with God's message.)

EXPLAIN that though we may not be called to interpret dreams or serve in government, we can serve in many ways that can influence others to consider Christ.

In Matthew 5:13-16 Jesus said, *"You are the salt of the earth, but if salt has lost its taste, how shall its saltiness be restored? It is no longer good for anything except to* *be thrown out and trampled under people's feet. You are the light of the world. A city set on a hill cannot be hidden. Nor do people light a lamp and put it under a basket, but on a stand, and it gives light to all in the house. In the same way, let your light shine before others, so that they may see your good works and give glory to your Father who is in heaven."*

In session 2, we considered what it means to be a spiritual light to those around us. What do you think it means that Jesus' followers are "*the salt of the earth*"? (If you have time, have students describe how Christians should display these traits.)

Salt seasons food—Christ's followers should enhance the society around them.

Salt is a preservative—Christ's followers should resist moral corruption and preserve godly influence on the culture.

Salt has healing properties—Christ's followers can help bring healing to people who are hurting physically, emotionally, and spiritually.

Salt creates thirst—Through serving and setting a good example, Christ's followers can give people a thirst to know more about God.

ILLUSTRATION: Display a glass of cold water with ice. Ask if it's possible to fish an ice cube from the water using a string. Then dip a thick string into the water and lay it across an ice cube. Sprinkle salt over the ice and string, and wait 30 seconds. You should be able to lift the ice out of the water with the string. Explain that the salt temporarily melts the ice, which then refreezes around the string.

- **How does this illustrate the effect Christians can have on non-Christians?** (A Christian's positive influence can melt away another person's coldness toward God and allow the Gospel message to take hold in his or her life. By humbly helping to meet people's practical needs, we are not just telling about Jesus, we are showing them what He's like.)

EXPLAIN that while Christlike behavior and an attitude of servanthood can help you gain favor and influence with some people, it will also bring opposition from others. **That's what happened with Daniel in the most well-known part of his story: Daniel in the lions' den.**

Daniel chapter 6 picks up shortly after the Medes and Persians had overtaken the Babylonians. Because of his exceptional character, abilities, and insight, Daniel had risen to a high position of leadership under previous Babylonian rulers. Under Darius the Mede, Daniel maintained his high position as one of three top leaders. When the king planned to set Daniel over the whole kingdom, the other administrators got jealous and set out to find fault with Daniel. But they couldn't find any trace of corruption. He was trustworthy in every way, and he wasn't negligent in any way.

- **Why are these character traits so vital for Jesus' followers?** (Christians should be known as highly trustworthy and conscientious people, reflecting God's truth and excellence. In serving Jesus, as in all aspects of life, our actions typically speak louder than our words.)

EXPLAIN that because they couldn't find any charge against Daniel, his jealous colleagues appealed to the king's pride and convinced him to make a law that no one could pray to anyone but the king for the next 30 days. Daniel had never hidden his faith, so the other administrators knew that this law would conflict with his loyalty to God.

HAVE students turn to the following passage in their Bibles or locate it on pages 56–57 in the Field Manual.

DANIEL 6:10–28: Read this passage—or allow two or three volunteers to take turns reading—as the class follows along.

- **Looking at Daniel 6:10–16, how did Daniel respond to the decree, and what does this reveal about his character, priorities, and devotion to God?** (He immediately went to God for help and even gave thanks. Though he was loyal in serving King Darius, the decree didn't take priority over God. Daniel realized the danger but didn't let anything keep him from time with God.)

EXPLAIN that from the way they "caught" Daniel praying, it was an obvious setup. They went to the king as a group to confirm that the law couldn't be repealed; then they revealed how Daniel had broken it. When the king realized what this meant, he regretted his decision and tried to save Daniel.

- **What does Daniel 6:16–19 indicate about the king's attitude toward Daniel and toward God?** (The king thought highly of Daniel because of his capabilities and dedication. He even expressed respect for Daniel's faith when he said, "*May your God, whom you serve continually, deliver you!*" [v. 16]. The king couldn't sleep that night, and at dawn he rushed to the lions' den and called out, "*O Daniel, servant of the living God, has your God, whom you serve continually, been able to deliver you from the lions?*" [v. 20].)

EXPLAIN that when Darius heard Daniel's voice, he was overjoyed and had Daniel lifted from the den. He then had Daniel's accusers thrown to the lions, and the lions immediately devoured them.

- **According to Daniel 6:25–27, what did the king say about God?** (He ordered everyone in the kingdom to honor Daniel's God as the living and eternal God. He credited God not only with saving Daniel, but with saving others and doing "*signs and wonders in heaven and on earth*" [v. 27].)

- **In the end, who was affected by Daniel's bold devotion to God?** (Just as Daniel's three friends had influenced the entire nation after the Lord rescued them from the fiery furnace, Daniel's rescue from the lions' den caused King Darius to make a decree that influenced the entire empire.)

EXPLAIN that because Daniel honored God even when facing life-threatening opposition, God honored him by miraculously rescuing him and giving him extraordinary influence. **Daniel impacted an entire kingdom because he faithfully served God and helped others. As we humbly serve God and help to meet others' needs—family members, teachers, church leaders, and those who can't always help themselves—God will open doors of opportunity to show and tell others about Jesus.**

HOLY BIBLE

BIBLE IN YOUR BRAIN
TIME: 5–10 minutes

MATERIALS NEEDED: Bibles and/or pages 58–59 in the student Field Manual (or Reproducible 4.4 from **D2BDTeacher.com**)

INVITE students to look at what else the Bible says about the personal sacrifice involved in following Jesus and how putting ourselves aside for the sake of others can help us reach them for Christ. (Have volunteers read the passages one at a time. Some of these you will recognize from the main teaching time. If you have time, briefly discuss the implications of each.)

(LEADER NOTE: Depending on your time frame, you may want to cover only a few of these passages, as students will cover most of them in brief devotional segments in their Field Manuals.)

Matthew 4:19-20
"And he said to them, 'Follow me, and I will make you fishers of men.' Immediately they left their nets and followed him."

Luke 9:23-26
"And he said to all, 'If anyone would come after me, let him deny himself and take up his cross daily and follow me. For whoever would save his life will lose it, but whoever loses his life for my sake will save it. For what does it profit a man if he gains the whole world and loses or forfeits himself? For whoever is ashamed of me and of my words, of him will the Son of Man be ashamed when he comes in his glory and the glory of the Father and of the holy angels.'"

Mark 10:42-45
"And Jesus called them to him and said to them, 'You know that those who are considered rulers of the Gentiles lord it over them, and their great ones exercise authority over them. But it shall not be so among you. But whoever would be great among you must be your servant, and whoever would be first among you must be slave of all. For even the Son of Man came not to be served but to serve, and to give his life as a ransom for many.'"

Matthew 5:13-16

"You are the salt of the earth, but if salt has lost its taste, how shall its saltiness be restored? It is no longer good for anything except to be thrown out and trampled under people's feet. You are the light of the world. A city set on a hill cannot be hidden. Nor do people light a lamp and put it under a basket, but on a stand, and it gives light to all in the house. In the same way, let your light shine before others, so that they may see your good works and give glory to your Father who is in heaven."

1 Peter 2:12

"Keep your conduct among the Gentiles honorable, so that when they speak against you as evildoers, they may see your good deeds and glorify God on the day of visitation."

1 John 3:16-18

"By this we know love, that [Jesus Christ] laid down his life for us, and we ought to lay down our lives for the brothers. But if anyone has the world's goods and sees his brother in need, yet closes his heart against him, how does God's love abide in him? Little children, let us not love in word or talk but in deed and in truth."

Colossians 3:12-14

"Put on then, as God's chosen ones, holy and beloved, compassionate hearts, kindness, humility, meekness, and patience, bearing with one another and, if one has a complaint against another, forgiving each other; as the Lord has forgiven you, so you also must forgive. And above all these put on love, which binds everything together in perfect harmony."

EXPLAIN that as followers of Jesus, our main mission is to influence others to follow Jesus. One of the most effective ways of doing that is to humbly meet people's needs in ways that reflect Jesus' love and make them more receptive to His message.

REFER students to pages 58–59 of the Field Manual, where they will find these passages, along with a practical challenge and prayer focus for each day of the coming week.

ACTIVITY ZONE
TIME: 5–10 minutes (Optional, depending on the session time frame)

OPTION 1: BACK BRIDGE
MATERIALS NEEDED: None

LINE UP students as quickly as possible according to height, from tallest to shortest. This doesn't need to be exact, so have them do it fast, perhaps to some upbeat music. If there are significant size differences (not just height), you may shift a few people a place or two forward or back, but don't do this if you think a person may be sensitive about weight. Have students count off by the number of teams you want. (You need at least five students per team.) If you have a large room and a large group, you may want fewer teams so that the human bridges they form will stretch farther across the room.

EXPLAIN that in this relay you'll see which team can get one of its members across the entire length of the room the fastest on a human bridge. Have all teams assemble on one side of the room and clear a path wide enough for all teams to get to the other side. Have each team determine their smallest, lightest member (who is willing to cross the bridge). The rest of the team will kneel down on all fours, side to side, forming a line that begins to stretch toward the other side of the room.

THE IDEA is for the smallest member to crawl on top of the backs of his or her kneeling teammates. After the bridge-crosser passes over people, he or she must get up from the back of the line and move to the front so the one crawling over can keep going continuously to the other side. If the bridge-crosser falls off or touches the floor, he or she must go back to the first person in line and start crawling over again.

ON "GO," both teams will start on the same side of the room and compete simultaneously to see which team can get their bridge-crosser to the other side of the room first.

POINT OUT that this relay illustrates how we can help bridge the gap between people and God. Of course, Jesus is the only One who could make a way for us to have a relationship with God. He bridged the gap between His Father and us by laying down His life to pay the price for our sin.

EXPLAIN that as Jesus' representatives, we can help people cross the "bridge" Christ provides. We can do this by serving people as well as sharing the message of Jesus. We can also "stand in the gap" by praying for people who don't know Jesus (cf. Ezekiel 22:30). The more we work together to help and serve people, the more effectively we can help them cross over from doubting God to trusting Him.

OPTION 2: PROGRESSIVE STORY
MATERIALS NEEDED: None

ASK students if they've ever told a progressive story. That's what they're going to do today. You wil start the story, and then go around the room so each person can add to the story. Here's the catch: When you add something, you must say something true about yourself.

START the story something like this: **Once upon a time, there was a young** (boy/girl: depends on your gender). **He loved to** (fill in with a favorite activity) **and tried to leave lots of time for this. One day, as he was on his way to the** (place to do this activity), **he met up with an old friend ...**

PASS the story on at this point. Remind the class they must include something true about themselves when they add on. Continue until everyone has had a chance to add to the story. When it comes back around to you, end it somehow—whether your ending makes a lot of sense or not! Sometimes "silly" is the best way to end a progressive story—so just say, "And they all lived happily ever after."

POINT OUT that in our progressive story, they all told something about themselves. Then allow for a few responses to this question: **Was it hard for you to add a part to this story? Why or why not?**

EXPLAIN that there will be times when the most effective way to share our faith is to tell our own stories of how God has worked in our individual lives. But above all we must still learn to tell the story of Jesus so that others can understand what He's done for them and why.

EMPHASIZE that Jesus' story involves all of us. And unlike the story we just made up, His story has a distinct purpose—to bring people into a personal relationship with God. While we must be prepared to tell the story of Jesus at any time, we can't just make up stuff as we go. We must be familiar with the message as God gives it to us in His Word. That's what we'll work on in a few moments.

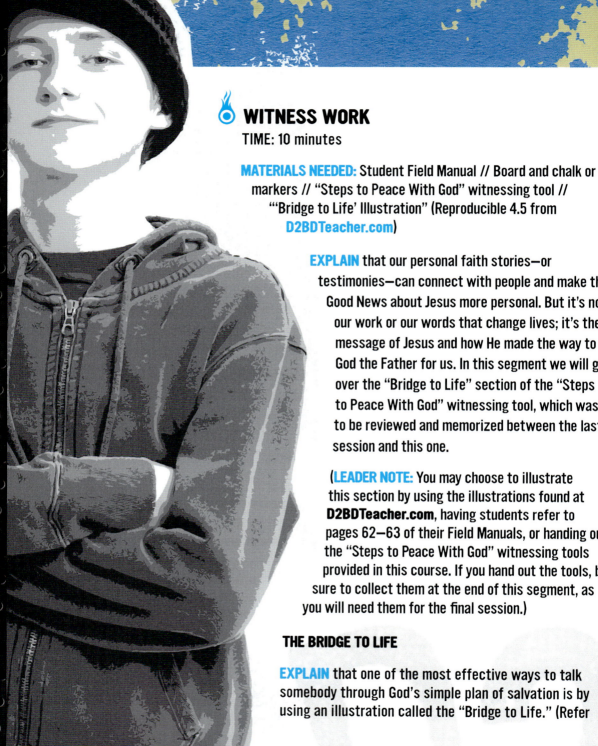

WITNESS WORK
TIME: 10 minutes

MATERIALS NEEDED: Student Field Manual // Board and chalk or markers // "Steps to Peace With God" witnessing tool // "'Bridge to Life' Illustration" (Reproducible 4.5 from D2BDTeacher.com)

EXPLAIN that our personal faith stories—or testimonies—can connect with people and make the Good News about Jesus more personal. But it's not our work or our words that change lives; it's the message of Jesus and how He made the way to God the Father for us. In this segment we will go over the "Bridge to Life" section of the "Steps to Peace With God" witnessing tool, which was to be reviewed and memorized between the last session and this one.

(**LEADER NOTE:** You may choose to illustrate this section by using the illustrations found at **D2BDTeacher.com**, having students refer to pages 62–63 of their Field Manuals, or handing out the "Steps to Peace With God" witnessing tools provided in this course. If you hand out the tools, be sure to collect them at the end of this segment, as you will need them for the final session.)

THE BRIDGE TO LIFE

EXPLAIN that one of the most effective ways to talk somebody through God's simple plan of salvation is by using an illustration called the "Bridge to Life." (Refer to Part 1 of the illustration.) **Most people around the world have a general awareness or belief that God exists and that because of the difference between His nature and ours, people are separated from Him. This separation actually exists because of *sin*, which is essentially the fact that we all choose to go our own way and fall short of God's perfect standard. In fact, sin is so radically opposed to God's perfect character that it requires the most extreme penalty: death and eternal separation from God.**

EMPHASIZE that though God loves us and created us to have a personal relationship with Him, His perfect character and justice cannot relate to or have fellowship with us in that condition. **The separation between people and God is as distinct as the contrast between full sunlight and complete darkness. They are mutually exclusive. It's as if there is a huge chasm or canyon between God and us.**

So where does that leave us in relation to God? **What can bridge the gap between sinful people and a holy God? Well, people have lots of theories about this. Some try to get to God by being good, going to church, or following a certain religion or philosophy. Does that work? No.** (Refer to Part 2 of the illustration.) **The truth is that the divide between people and God is so wide that no human idea or effort—no matter how "good"—can bridge that gap. It would be like trying to jump the Grand Canyon. Even the longest jumper in the world would plummet over the edge and fall to certain death.**

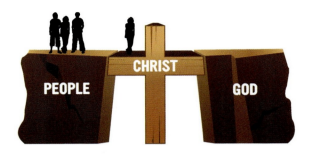

Then how do we bridge this great divide and relate to God as He created us to do? **We can't—we needed God to do something to rescue us from the consequences of sin. So here's what He did. Because He loves us so much, instead of sentencing us to death as our sins deserve, God sent His Son to become human, to live a sinless life, and to die in our place. Though Jesus didn't deserve death, He took on our sins—our penalty—when He was executed on the cross. But because He was without sin, death had no claim on Christ—it couldn't hold Him—so He rose from the dead. Jesus' life now bridges the gap between God and humanity.**

1 Timothy 2:5 **says,** *"For there is one God, and there is one mediator between God and men, the man Christ Jesus."*

1 Peter 3:18 **says,** *"For Christ also suffered once for sins, the righteous for the unrighteous, that he might bring us to God, being put to death in the flesh but made alive in the spirit."*

Now everyone who believes this—who puts their trust not in what they can do to solve their sin problem, but in what Jesus did for us—can be connected with God. (Refer to Part 3 of the illustration.) **This is why the symbol of the cross is so important to Christians. It's a reminder that we have peace with God not because of what we do, but because of what God did for us when He sent His only Son, Jesus, to die on the cross for us.**

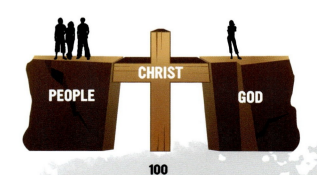

BREAK into pairs or small groups and have students practice explaining the "Bridge to Life" illustration in their own words.

HIGHLIGHT Step 4 of the "Steps to Peace With God" witnessing tool, along with the related Bible verses that they'll memorize between now and the next session. By this time, students have covered all four steps, although they may not have everything down yet. Still, they'll benefit from practicing the Gospel presentation from start to finish between now and the next session.

CHALLENGE students to practice sharing the "Steps to Peace With God" process—particularly the "Bridge to Life" illustration—with someone outside of class between now and the next session. They should explain each step using the related Bible verses. As one partner presents the message, the other partner can ask simple questions—as if he or she is a non-Christian who is ready to receive the message. The second partner should not try to stump the first partner, however, as he or she practices. **They will record their experiences on page 66 of the student Field Manual.**

REFER students to page 65 in their Field Manuals. Point out that the "Step by Step" section outlines a process of sharing Jesus' message that they need to review in preparation for the final session, when they will practice this entire process.

RESPONDING THROUGH RELATIONSHIP:

In a survey, 10,000 Christians were asked about how they came to Christ and to their church*:

0.5% attended a revival service • 1% visited a church on their own • 2% had a special need that brought them there • 3% just walked in • 3% liked the church programs offered
5% came for the Sunday school • 6% liked the pastor • 79% were invited by a friend or relative

As you can see, the greatest number of people who come to Christ respond to the Gospel through an already-established relationship.

*STUDENT DISCIPLESHIP MINISTRIES

THE OWN-ZONE
TIME: 5 minutes

MATERIALS NEEDED: Student Field Manual and/or "It's Your Serve" (Reproducible 4.6 from D2BDTeacher.com) // Pens or pencils

HAVE students turn to page 60 in their Field Manuals, where they will find the section entitled "It's Your Serve." (If they don't have manuals, distribute copies of Reproducible 4.6.) Give them a few minutes to look over the headings and examples in each of the following categories:

- Friends
- School
- Community
- Family
- People who don't know Jesus

ENCOURAGE students to think of simple, practical ways they could serve people in each of those contexts and to write these ideas in their Field Manuals. (Have them come up with at least one or two ideas for each category. They'll be able to add to their lists between now and the next session.) Pay particular attention to ideas for serving people who don't know Jesus in ways that might draw their attention to God and cause them to consider a relationship with Him.

ALLOW a couple minutes for students to pray, asking God to help them recognize opportunities to serve and to help them follow through in the ways they listed.

 THE DANIEL DARE
TIME: 5–10 minutes

MATERIALS NEEDED: Student Field Manual (or Reproducible 4.7, "Daniel Dare" for session 4, from **D2BDTeacher.com**)

REFER students to pages 66–67 in the Field Manual. (If they don't have manuals, distribute copies of Reproducible 4.7.) If you have extended time, students can start on this exercise now; otherwise, briefly describe what they'll do outside of class.

EXPLAIN that between now and the next session, they'll practice something that should become a normal way of life. They're going to be on the alert and ready to help, serve, and meet needs. This includes helping family at home, assisting ministry leaders, showing active compassion for people in need, and performing random acts of kindness wherever they are.

CHALLENGE students not to wait to be asked to do things, but to take the initiative by volunteering to help anyone we can. Emphasize the need to serve and show kindness without expecting something in return. **We should look for opportunities to**

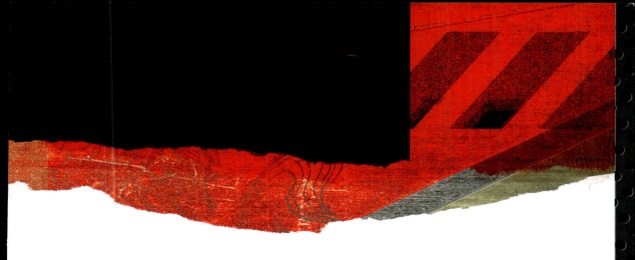

start conversations with those we serve—especially if they ask questions. We should always look for ways to draw attention to God.

- **How could we bring God into the conversations with people we help and serve?** (We could be direct and say, "God's been good to me, and I want to pass that on." Or we could be more subtle, like bringing church into the conversation if people start talking about things in which they're involved. We could even mention that we're participating in this class, which challenged us to be more helpful. Any of these things could lead to deeper conversations about faith and God.)

ASK students to note in their Field Manuals some of the opportunities they have to serve and what they are able to talk to people about as a result. Encourage them to be prepared to share what they experienced in following through on this "Daniel Dare."

CLOSING
TIME: 5 minutes

REMIND students that their actions often speak louder than their words. That's why it's so important to do what God wants them to do. In fact, *they can point others to Christ by following His example of self-sacrifice and humble service.* As they obey God in every aspect of life—public and private—they will have opportunities to share their faith.

ENCOURAGE students to follow through on their plans to serve friends, families, schools, and communities in ways that will help people become more receptive to the message of Jesus.

ASK for a volunteer or two to close in prayer, or lead students in the following prayer:

Dear Jesus, thank You for the ultimate sacrifice You made for me so I could be forgiven and live forever with You. Help me put myself aside and follow You with all my heart so I can fulfill Your plans for me. Help me always to be humble. Show me how I can meet others' needs in ways that show Your love and draw attention to You. Help me to serve You faithfully in every aspect of life—private and public. Don't let anything keep me from time with You. Continually search my heart to reveal what needs to change to strengthen my faith and witness. I ask this in Your Name, Jesus. Amen.

DON'T FORGET the memory work, daily devotions, and "Daniel Dare" in the student Field Manual. Be prepared to share your progress in the next session.

Dare to Be a Witness

Key Focus: A clear presentation of the message of Jesus is essential for people to receive the forgiveness and new life He offers. This is Good News that people need to hear and we must be prepared to tell.

 SESSION OVERVIEW

"I've got some good news and some bad news." When that familiar line is used to introduce a joke, people always want to hear both sides of the situation. But real life is no joke, and we would much rather get the good news and forget the bad. In an age where bad news saturates society and emanates from every corner of the globe, a good report can be as settling as a candle in a dark room. The ultimate Good News—a message so positive and powerful that it can dispel even the darkest situation—is the message of how Jesus provided forgiveness and eternal life to all who willingly receive these gifts.

Over the last few sessions, looking at the lives of Daniel and his friends, we've considered how our own words, actions, and lifestyle can affect our influence for God. But while our experience may cause people to consider who God is, what He's like, and what He can do, only the message of Jesus can truly transform their lives. Yet, in order for people to believe and receive the Good News of Jesus, they must hear, understand, and relate to it. That's why *a clear presentation of the message of Jesus is essential for people to receive the forgiveness and new life He offers.*

This final study in the *Dare to Be a Daniel Experience* series focuses on the actual delivery of the Good News that Jesus commands His followers to go and tell (see Mark 16:15). Through this session, students will review some key principles from past studies and put together all the pieces of the Gospel presentation. By now, the hope is that your students believe that this is news so good they can't keep it to themselves.

Through this session, students will learn to:

- Understand that the Good News about Jesus is the only message that can truly transform lives.
- Realize that people must understand and relate to Jesus' message in order to receive it.
- Accept Jesus' command to boldly tell others about Him.
- Be prepared to graciously and respectfully share Jesus' message with all who are willing to listen.
- Practice giving a clear, concise presentation of the Good News about Jesus.

PLANNING & PREP

For this session, you'll need:

1. Student Field Manuals (one per student)
2. Bibles (one per student)
3. Paper and pens/pencils for all students
4. Reproducibles for Lesson 5 from **D2BDTeacher.com**
5. *The Reel World* DVD (clip 5)
6. Slips of paper with bad news scenarios
7. Large cloth tarp or sheet // Two poles or stands // Tape // Slips of paper and pencils // "Foot" prize or shoe trophy
8. Beach ball or large paper wad
9. Prizes for shoe search winners (e.g., candy or shoe laces)
10. Small jigsaw puzzles // Small prizes
11. "Steps to Peace With God" witnessing tool (one per student)

 JUMP-START THEIR HEARTS
TIME: 5–10 minutes

OPTION 1: BAD NEWS/GOOD NEWS
MATERIALS NEEDED: Slips of paper with bad news scenarios

EXPLAIN that we've all heard jokes that start with "I have some good news and some bad news." Have students get into pairs or small groups and give each group one of the following bad news scenarios. (You might need to come up with a few of your own, depending on class size.)

- You lost your mom's cellphone.
- You accidentally started a fire in the garage.
- You didn't make the team you worked so hard to get on.
- You overheard someone spreading a false rumor about you.
- Your "friend" told someone that you like him or her, and the other person just laughed.
- You scored a 63 on your English midterm.
- Your best friend just informed you that he or she is moving.

GIVE groups a couple minutes to create a good news scenario (serious or silly) that would change the outlook on the situation to a more positive one. Have someone in each group tell the class the good news that changed his or her bad news. Then discuss the following questions:

- **What kind of power or effect can good news have? How can good news turn a situation around?**

EXPLAIN that we might want to hear both sides of a good news/bad news joke. But in real life, people typically prefer to get good news and forget the bad. **The right good news can even "undo" bad news and turn our perspective of a situation completely around. That's the power of the Good News of Jesus. But in order for His message to change people, they have to hear, understand, and respond to it. That's why it's vital for us to be able to explain who Jesus is, why He came, what He did, what that means, and how to respond.**

(Go to FOLLOW-UP section for both options 1 and 2.)

110

OPTION 2: BEAUTIFUL FEET CONTEST

MATERIALS NEEDED: Large cloth tarp or sheet // Two poles or stands // Tape // Slips of paper and pencils // "Foot" prize or shoe trophy // Bibles

BEFORE THE SESSION: Suspend a sheet or tarp between two poles about six feet high, concealing several chairs. (Two extended microphone stands with a sheet hung between them or two volunteers holding a tarp will do.)

ANNOUNCE that you're having a "Beautiful Feet Contest" and ask three to seven volunteers to sit in chairs behind the curtain, which should conceal their identities. Have them remove their shoes and socks. Then lift the curtain just high enough to expose the volunteers' feet. Tape numbers on the floor in front of each contestant and have the class serve as judges. As students pass in front of the curtain, have them vote for the best-looking feet by writing the corresponding number on a small slip of paper. Tally the votes and announce one winner.

AWARD the winner a prize, such as a set of odor-eating foam insoles, foot cream, or a trophy made of an old shoe nailed to a block of wood and spray painted gold.

READ or have a volunteer read Romans 10:13–15 while the class follows along. Ask students to pay particular attention to the chain of events described in this passage.

"For, 'everyone who calls on the name of the Lord will be saved.' How then will they call on him in whom they have not believed? And how are they to believe in him of whom they have never heard? And how are they to hear without someone preaching? And how are they to preach unless they are sent? As it is written, 'How beautiful are the feet of those who preach the good news!'"

- **According to this passage, what chain of events enables someone to come to Jesus and be saved?** (Sending, preaching, hearing, believing, calling on the Lord.)

EXPLAIN that in order for His message to change people, they have to hear, understand, and respond to it. That's why it's vital for us to be able to explain who Jesus is, why He came, what He did, what that means, and how to respond.

FOLLOW-UP for both options 1 and 2:

READ or have a volunteer read Romans 10:9–13 while the class follows along.

"Because, if you confess with your mouth that Jesus is Lord and believe in your heart that God raised him from the dead, you will be saved. For with the heart one believes and is justified, and with the mouth one confesses and is saved. For the Scripture says, 'Everyone who believes in him will not be put to shame.' For there is no distinction between Jew and Greek; for the same Lord is Lord of all, bestowing his riches on all who call on him. For 'everyone who calls on the name of the Lord will be saved.'"

- **According to this passage, what does a person have to do to be saved?** (Confess that Jesus is Lord, believe He was raised from the dead, trust in Him, and call on the Lord.)

- **What does all this mean—to confess, believe, trust, and call? Is any of it difficult? Explain.** (The process is as simple as it sounds. The Bible is clear. It's not meant to be difficult for a person to receive the forgiveness, salvation, and new life that Christ offers.)

EXPLAIN that although it may seem difficult at times to communicate Christ's message and live a Christian life in today's world, God has made it relatively simple to receive His gift of salvation and eternal life. **The hard part isn't calling on Jesus; the real effort should be put into spreading the message.** *A clear presentation of the message of Jesus is essential for people to receive the forgiveness and new life He offers.*

In this final study of the *Dare to Be a Daniel Experience* series, we will review key points from past studies and put together the pieces of the Gospel presentation. *That's Good News that people need to hear and we must be prepared to tell.*

 INSTANT REPLAY

TIME: 5 minutes

MATERIALS NEEDED: Student Field Manual or "Instant Replay Discussion Guide" (Reproducible 5.1 from D2BDTeacher.com)

DIVIDE the class into pairs or threes. Refer to last session's "Daniel Dare" on pages 66–67 of the student Field Manual and/or distribute copies of the "Instant Replay Discussion Guide" for session 5. Have students briefly share with their partners two or three opportunities they had to help and serve others and what they were able to talk to people about as a result.

ENCOURAGE students to offer each other feedback regarding how they might have directed their conversations differently with the people they helped, to influence them even more for Christ.

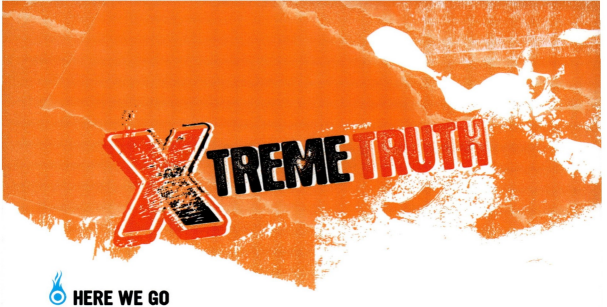

🔥 HERE WE GO

TIME: 20–25 minutes (including the main Bible reading)

MATERIALS NEEDED: Beach ball or large paper wad

IMPORTANT LEADER NOTE: Unless you have an extended time period, you will *not* be able to cover all of the material in this main teaching session. The segmented format with blue directives allows you to pick and choose the paragraphs, portions, questions, illustrations, etc., that are best suited to your class and time frame. The material here is not intended to be used word for word, but simply to provide direction so you can convey the content in your own style.

Mark 16:15; 1 Peter 3:15

READ or have a volunteer read Mark 16:15 while the class follows along.

"[Jesus] said to them, 'Go into all the world and proclaim the gospel to the whole creation.'"

ASK students if they know what this passage is often called. Point out that this is one version of what's commonly known as the Great Commission.

EXPLAIN that this was Jesus' final command before leaving earth and returning to heaven following His death and resurrection. **The message of Jesus is Good News that's meant to be shared because it is the only message that can truly transform lives. Jesus told His followers to go everywhere and tell people about Him. This isn't a request or suggestion, but a direct command.**

EMPHASIZE that we must be prepared to tell people the Good News about Jesus and how people can find forgiveness, hope, and eternal life through faith in Him.

- In what ways can the Good News about Jesus change lives?

READ or have a volunteer read 1 Peter 3:15 while the class follows along.

"But in your hearts revere Christ as Lord. Always be prepared to give an answer to everyone who asks you to give the reason for the hope that you have. But do this with gentleness and respect" (NIV).

EXPLAIN that the word *prepared* means "ready, willing, and equipped." It implies being ready to meet any challenge that comes along.

- **Why should you always be ready to talk about the hope you have in Christ? What might cause a person to ask you about it?** (You never know when you might encounter someone who needs and is ready to hear about Jesus. If you're living, acting, and speaking in ways that reflect hope and a positive difference, someone is bound to ask about it at some point. Also, people who are skeptical about your faith might confront you with questions.)

- **According to this verse, how should you respond to questions and challenges about your faith?** (We are to "*do this with gentleness and respect.*") **Why is it important?** (Most people resist a confrontational or argumentative response. It's unconvincing and actually turns people off when Christians seem stubborn, closed-minded, or obnoxious. By being respectful, we're more likely to be heard and perhaps develop a relationship through which we can influence people to consider Christ for themselves. Also, being kind and considerate reflects Christ's love and character.)

EXPLAIN that it's one thing to talk about being ready to respond—but it's another thing to actually be prepared. **Let's play a quick game that illustrates how tough it can be to respond to questions at a moment's notice.**

ACTIVITY OPTION: THINK ON YOUR FEET

Sometimes you need to think on your feet. If you had to give a speech at school or a short message in youth group, you would probably have a little time to prepare. But life isn't always so kind as to allow prep time, so let's see how you are at thinking on your feet. I'll shout out a question and then toss this beach ball (or paper wad) to someone. As soon as you catch it, you have to answer the question—even if you drop the ball. Once you answer

the question, toss the ball to someone who hasn't had it yet. As you do, I'll shout another question, which that person will have to answer. Have students stand in a circle, then toss the ball to one of them and ask that student the first question. Play for only about five minutes, or until everyone has had a turn. Here are several questions. Feel free to add your own.

- **Why should I follow Jesus Christ?**
- **All religions are basically the same, right? Why or why not?**
- **If God is so good, why is there so much evil and suffering in the world?**
- **Wasn't Jesus just a prophet or a good teacher?**
- **I'm basically a good person—that's enough to get to heaven, right?**
- **The Bible isn't all true, is it?**
- **How could a loving God send anyone to hell?**
- **Why would I want to follow God when none of my friends do?**

AFTER playing for about five minutes, discuss the following questions if time allows:

- **How or why was it hard to answer quickly?**
- **At what other times do you have a hard time thinking of what to say?**
- **What could you do to make it easier to reply to questions like these?**

EXPLAIN that it's not easy to find the right words or Bible verses on the spur of the moment. And we can never be sure how long we'll have to respond to someone. Putting some thought and preparation into how we would respond, however, will make it easier to speak up when opportunities arise.

REMIND students how Shadrach, Meshach, and Abednego responded boldly and without hesitation after refusing to bow to the king's idol (Daniel 3). In the same way, we need to be ready to respond, whether the challenges come from people who are open to our faith or opposed to it.

- **Why were these young men so bold, and how were they spared from the fiery furnace?** (You may recall how they said, "*Our God whom we serve is able to deliver us from the* *burning fiery furnace, and he will deliver us out of your hand*" [Daniel 3:17]. As it turned out, God was with them and protected them through the fire. God can do the same for you.)

In Matthew 28:19–20, another version of Jesus' Great Commission, He concludes with a promise: ***"Go therefore and make disciples of all nations, baptizing them in the name of the Father and of the Son and of the Holy Spirit, teaching them to observe all that I have commanded you. And behold, I am with you always, to the end of the age."***

- **What assurance does Jesus give in this passage?** (He promised to always be with those who are actively involved in spreading His message and influencing others to follow Him.)

EXPLAIN that if Jesus is with us, we don't have to be afraid of what others can do to us and we don't have to worry about what to say.

POINT OUT that on several occasions Daniel received supernatural insight from God that allowed him to respond to kings' requests (Daniel chapter 1), interpret dreams (chapters 2 and 4), explain unusual events (chapter 5), and give godly counsel. While we may not be called to do these exact things, Jesus promises to help us, even in the most difficult situations.

In Matthew 10:18–20, Jesus tells His followers, ***"And you will be dragged before governors and kings for my sake, to bear witness before them and the Gentiles. When they deliver you over, do not be anxious how you are to speak or what you are to say, for what you are to say will be given to you in that hour. For it is not you who speak, but the Spirit of your Father speaking through you."***

EXPLAIN that Jesus promises that when we speak up about our faith in Him, the Holy Spirit will guide us in what to say. **Our part is to develop a deeper relationship with God so we become sensitive to His voice. Also, if we're faithful to learn Bible passages that can help us communicate our faith, then the Holy Spirit can bring them to mind at the time. This will help us clearly present the message of Jesus, which is essential for people to receive the forgiveness and new life He offers.**

Before this session is over, you'll have an opportunity to practice the things you've learned about sharing your faith in Jesus and leading others into a personal relationship with Him.

BIBLE IN YOUR BRAIN
TIME: 5–10 minutes

MATERIALS NEEDED: Bible and/or pages 76–77 in the student Field Manual (or Reproducible 5.3 from D2BDTeacher.com)

LET'S LOOK at what else the Bible says about boldly sharing your faith in Jesus and influencing others to follow Him. (Have volunteers read the passages one at a time. Some of these you will recognize from the main teaching time. If you have time, briefly discuss the implications of each.)

(**LEADER NOTE:** Depending on your time frame, you may want to cover only a few of these passages, as students will cover most of them in brief devotional segments in their Field Manuals.)

Romans 10:9-15
"Because, if you confess with your mouth that Jesus is Lord and believe in your heart that God raised him from the dead, you will be saved. For with the heart one believes and is justified, and with the mouth one confesses and is saved. For the Scripture says, 'Everyone who believes in him will not be put to shame.' For there is no distinction between Jew and Greek; for the same Lord is Lord of all, bestowing his riches on all who call on him. For 'everyone who calls on the name of the Lord will be saved.' How then will they call on him in whom they have not believed? And how are they to believe in him of whom they have never heard? And how are they to hear without someone preaching? And how are they to preach unless they are sent? As it is written, 'How beautiful are the feet of those who preach the good news!'"

Matthew 28:19-20
"Go therefore and make disciples of all nations, baptizing them in the name of the Father and of the Son and of the Holy Spirit, teaching them to observe all that I have commanded you. And behold, I am with you always, to the end of the age."

1 Peter 3:15, NIV

"But in your hearts revere Christ as Lord. Always be prepared to give an answer to everyone who asks you to give the reason for the hope that you have. But do this with gentleness and respect."

2 Timothy 1:7

"For God gave us a spirit not of fear but of power and love and self-control."

1 John 1:9

"If we confess our sins, he is faithful and just to forgive us our sins and to cleanse us from all unrighteousness."

1 John 5:12-13

"Whoever has the Son has life; whoever does not have the Son of God does not have life."

EXPLAIN that God hasn't made it difficult to receive His gift of salvation and eternal life—but a person must hear and respond to the Good News about Jesus in order to experience the benefits of a personal relationship with God. **That's why *Jesus' followers must be prepared to give a clear presentation of the message of Jesus, so people can receive the forgiveness and new life He offers.***

REFER students to pages 76–77 of the Field Manual, where they will find these passages, along with a practical challenge and prayer focus for each day of the coming week.

 ACTIVITY ZONE
TIME: 5–10 minutes

OPTION 1: SHOE SLEUTHS
MATERIALS NEEDED: Prize(s) for contest winners

HAVE all students remove both of their shoes and mix them up in a pile on one side of the room. Then have students form pairs so that each one is with someone they don't know very well. One person in each pair will be the "detective." When you say go, the second person in each pair will describe his or her shoes to their detective, who must then run to find them in the shoe pile and return them to their owner. If the detective brings back the wrong shoes, he or she must gather more clues and then search again. If the detective brings back the right shoes, the owner puts them on and then becomes the detective.

REPEAT the process until one team finds all of their shoes. (Or, if you have time, play until you have several winners or until everyone has their shoes.) Offer small prizes—such as candy or a wild pair of shoelaces—to members of the winning team. Then discuss the following questions:

- **Did you find it difficult to describe your shoes to someone who didn't know what they looked like? Why or why not?**

- **How is describing your shoes to someone similar to presenting the Gospel?**

- **What might happen if we don't present the message clearly?**

- **How can we become more effective in sharing Jesus with others, even this week?**

EXPLAIN that many people are searching for something and they may not even realize that only Christ can provide it for them. **If we don't clearly communicate—both by action and words—what Jesus is like, they may not see what they're looking for. A clear presentation of the message of Jesus is essential for people to receive the forgiveness and new life He offers. This is Good News that people need to hear and we must be prepared to tell.**

OPTION 2: GET IT TOGETHER
MATERIALS NEEDED: Small jigsaw puzzles (one for each small group) // Small prizes

BRING to class two or more small jigsaw puzzles (about 50 pieces each). Divide the class into groups of five or six—perhaps by guys and girls. Give each group an unassembled puzzle in a blank envelope, but don't give them the box with the picture of the completed puzzle. When you say, "Go," have the groups race to see who can assemble the puzzle the fastest. Award small prizes to the group that finishes first. Then briefly discuss the following questions:

- **Was assembling the puzzles easy or difficult, and why?** (It was likely more difficult without seeing the whole picture beforehand.)

- **How could putting the puzzle together be compared with sharing the Gospel with people?** (It's not always easy. Each situation can be a little different. It has several elements, and when everything comes together, it makes sense and is complete.)

EXPLAIN that over the past several weeks, we've studied and practiced a number of skills involved in communicating the message of Jesus on a personal level and leading others into a relationship with Him. In this final session, we'll put all the pieces together and consider what to do when a person gets the picture and is prepared to respond to the message.

THE REEL WORLD, SCENE 5, THE ONE WITH THE GIRL TALKING ABOUT RELIGION

TIME: 15–20 minutes

MATERIALS NEEDED: DVD // "Reel World Discussion Guide" (Reproducible 5.2, from **D2BDTeacher.com**)

PLAY *The Reel World*, clip 5, "Dare to Be a Witness." Lindsey is just hanging out with the girls. All of a sudden, a discussion breaks out on religion. Statements like "all religions are really the same" and "it's just a crutch for weak people" open the door for Lindsey to share her faith. Will she take the opportunity and be a witness?

After the video, discuss the following questions using the "Reel World Discussion Guide" for clip 5:

- **What would you say in this situation?**

- **What happens if she does nothing or changes the subject?**

WITNESS WORK

TIME: 10 minutes

MATERIALS NEEDED: Student Field Manual and/or "Witness Work" outline (Reproducible 5.4, from **D2BDTeacher.com**) // "Steps to Peace With God" witnessing tool

EXPLAIN that regardless of how God uses us to influence others, Scripture makes it clear that we can't save or "convert" anyone. Only God can truly transform a heart and life. But if we'll communicate what we know and have experienced, we can help people discover the need for God and for the new life Christ provides.

REFER students to pages 78–79 in their Field Manuals. (If they don't have manuals, use Reproducible 5.4, "Witness Work" outline, from **D2BDTeacher.com**.) Since the last session, they've reviewed and familiarized themselves with the process they might follow in sharing their faith and leading someone into a relationship with Jesus. By now they've also practiced most of these elements separately, both in and out of class.

AT THIS TIME they'll have the opportunity to put all the pieces together and practice an entire presentation. Though they may still be a little shaky with their delivery, encourage them to refer to the process outline no more than necessary to stay on track.

- **Develop common ground.**
- **Use a transitional statement.**
- **Share your story with the person.**
- **Ask if he or she would like to know how to become a Christian.**

- **Present the Gospel, using Scripture and illustrations.**
- **Ask the person if he or she is ready to trust Christ.**
- **Lead the person in prayer.**
- **Show him or her verses on the assurance of salvation.**
- **Show him or her where to start reading in the Bible.**

HAVE students get into pairs and take turns going through the entire process, with one partner filling the role of the Christian and the other partner listening in the role of a non-Christian who is ready to hear about Jesus. Students should get a turn to play each role. Encourage them to interact throughout the process and to use the "Steps to Peace With God" witnessing tool as the basis for presenting God's plan of salvation.

START this exercise by having the partners pick a topic of conversation that could allow for a transition to the subject of faith, God, or a relationship with Jesus. (Refer to "Conversational Connections" on pages 42–44 of the student Field Manual.) Pretend that the conversation has already reached that point, so the students sharing the Gospel can start with a transitional statement and then ask their partner if they could tell about their own experience with God (their personal testimony).

ENCOURAGE students that while this exercise may in some ways seem awkward and unrealistic, it will help them get more comfortable with all the main elements of a Gospel presentation. As they become more comfortable and fluid in their presentations, they'll be able to tailor them more naturally to their own wording and style.

Since this is the final session of the D2BD course—and this exercise is vital—allow students to continue practicing into the time normally allotted for personal reflection in "The Own-Zone."

THE OWN-ZONE

TIME: 5 minutes

MATERIALS NEEDED: None

ALLOW students to continue practicing the Gospel presentation until all students have had the opportunity to go through the entire process.

INVITATION: If there happen to be students in the class who have not yet made the decision to follow Jesus, provide an opportunity for them to respond to the message they have just heard. Lead them in prayer as they surrender and entrust their lives to Jesus as the Forgiver of their sins and Leader of their lives. (Note: Use the sample prayer on the included "Steps to Peace With God" witnessing tool to help guide this time if needed.)

 THE DANIEL DARE
TIME: 5–10 minutes

MATERIALS NEEDED: Student Field Manual (or Reproducible 5.5, "Daniel Dare" for session 5, from **D2BDTeacher.com**)

REFER students to pages 82–83 in the Field Manual. (If they don't have manuals, distribute copies of Reproducible 5.5.) If you have an extended time, students can start on this exercise now; otherwise, briefly describe what they'll do outside of class.

CHALLENGE students with the fact that they've now learned to tell the story of their own experience with Christ and to convey the most important message possible—the Good News that we can have a personal relationship with God and live with Him forever because of what His Son, Jesus, has done for us. They've also practiced these skills in the controlled classroom setting. But now it's time to do these things for real.

EXPLAIN that the final "Daniel Dare" is an ongoing challenge to apply what they've learned from this course by putting it into practice in real-life situations. Remind them that the Holy Spirit is with them and will give them the words to say at the right time if they rely on Him.

THIS WEEK, students will pray for the friends with whom they've wanted to share Christ. They'll also ask God to help them recognize and respond to opportunities to talk about their faith. On pages 88–89 of the student Field Manual, they will answer the following:

- **Who did you talk to?**
- **What happened?**
- **What's your next move?**
- **How will you pray?**

CLOSING
TIME: 5 minutes

REMIND students that the truth about Jesus is the only message that can truly transform lives. But in order for people to receive the message, they must understand and relate to it. For this reason, a clear presentation of the message of Jesus is essential for people to receive the forgiveness and new life He offers. That's why we must prepare to share the Good News of Jesus.

JESUS HIMSELF has called us to that mission, and He's equipped us to fulfill it in the power of His Holy Spirit. We have no need to fear what others may think or do as we graciously share Christ's hope with all who are willing to hear.

ENCOURAGE students to continually "practice" presenting their faith story by telling anyone who is willing to listen about their personal experience with Jesus. Challenge them to become more comfortable in conveying God's plan of salvation by continually reviewing the "Steps to Peace With God" witnessing tool and by keeping the related Bible passages fresh in their memories. Carrying one or two of these tracts with them at all times will help.

ASK for a volunteer or two to close in prayer, or lead students in the following prayer:

Dear Jesus, I thank You for the opportunity to take part in training like this, which will help me become better equipped to lead others into a personal relationship with You. Thank You for the eternal impact that this will have on my life and on others whom I can influence for You. Thank You for not leaving me alone but sending your Holy Spirit to guide and empower me to witness for You. I trust You to give me the right words at the right time to defend my faith and help others understand Your truth. I pray for people I know who still lack a personal relationship with You. Use me in any way You choose to lead these individuals to You. I ask this in Your Name, Jesus. Amen.

CHALLENGE students to review all of the memory verses and "Witness Work" in their Field Manuals and to read over the list of "99 Ways to Be a Witness" on page 132. They should also be familiar with the follow-up measures for people who receive Christ. These are listed on page 81 of the student Field Manual, as well as at the end of the "Steps to Peace With God" witnessing tool. Make sure that every student has at least a couple of these tracts to take with them.

(LEADER NOTE: Schedule a time for a commissioning service to cap off this training course.)

D2BD COMMISSIONING SERVICE

(Use this as the culmination of this training course and a launching point for students into a life of adventurous service for God.)

MATERIALS NEEDED: Completion certificates (Reproducible from **D2BDTeacher.com**)

Remember, send in your students' information on the completion form provided or by using **D2BDTeacher.com** so that they can receive their personalized ID card and dog tags.*

BEFORE THE SERVICE: Print out and complete a commissioning certificate for each student. Consider printing these in color on white, heavyweight paper.

READ or have a student read 1 Peter 3:15: *"But in your hearts revere Christ as Lord. Always be prepared to give an answer to everyone who asks you to give the reason for the hope that you have. But do this with gentleness and respect'"* (NIV).

EXPLAIN to those present that your students have accepted the challenge of this Bible passage. They have been faithful to prepare themselves to respond to others who may have questions about God. Not only that; they have decided to become proactive in looking for opportunities to share the love and message of Jesus in words and actions.

CALL students up one by one and present them with their commissioning certificate. (Read what the certificate says so that those present know what the students are receiving.) When students come forward, you can also give them a copy of the completion form.

GIVE your students a final charge, asking them to accept each of the following challenges by responding: "We will."

- **Will you dare to be different—purposing in your heart to do what God wants you to do, regardless of what those around you are doing?** (We will.)

- **Will you dare to be disciplined—committing to pray and spend time in God's Word daily, so you can learn to recognize God's voice and put God's plans into practice?** (We will.)

*Note—If you would like to receive your students' personalized completion kits from Team D2BD to use in your commissioning service, be sure to send your form in early and check the appropriate box.

- **Will you dare to be discerning—picking godly friends who encourage you to stand firm in faith, even in the face of intense opposition?** (We will.)

- **Will you dare to be devoted—pointing others to God by what you say and do in all aspects of life, public and private?** (We will.)

- **Will you dare to share your faith—boldly pursuing opportunities to tell others about the life-transforming message of forgiveness and new life through faith in Jesus Christ?** (We will.)

AFTER students have responded to these challenges, sing a hymn, chorus, or Christian song that the group enjoys and that fits with the theme of telling others about Christ. Some students like to sing along with tracks of their favorite artists on CD. Do what fits best with your group.

CLOSE by asking students to join you in a commissioning prayer like this:

Almighty God, we thank You for sending Your Son, Jesus Christ, and for the great gift of salvation You've given us through Him. We thank You for the wisdom, guidance, and inspiration of Your Word, and for the presence of the Holy Spirit, who is with us as we share the message of Jesus with others. Now I ask Your blessing on each student here. Empower them to share the Good News boldly and to practice Your Word obediently. Go before them in every opportunity to influence someone for You. Equip them for every good work in Christ Jesus through Your Spirit. Thank You for all You've taught us through this course, and use us for Your honor. We ask this in Jesus' Name. Amen.

99 WAYS TO BE A WITNESS

There are a lot of ways to be salt and light (see Matthew 5:13–16) on your campus. Below are some ways you can be a positive example and provide an authentic Christian influence that may cause others to consider the claims of Christ for themselves. Some ideas may require you to be more verbal about your faith than others. Pray about your approach, and the Lord will show you how to be His light.

1. Develop a reputation as a genuinely friendly person.
2. Befriend those whom others avoid or ridicule.
3. Be a person of integrity.
4. Be a good listener.
5. Be sensitive, always looking for opportunities to help and encourage those who are lonely or hurting.
6. Be respectful of those in authority, even when others are not.
7. Say something nice about someone whom others are taunting or belittling.
8. Keep a good attitude in all situations.
9. Write notes of encouragement to friends. Include Bible verses that apply to challenges they are facing.
10. Be respectful to school staff.
11. Pray over your meals.
12. Pray for other students.
13. Meet with Christian friends at your locker, flagpole, or other designated locations for prayer every morning.
14. Organize a "See You at the Pole" prayer meeting for the fourth Wednesday in September.
15. Be prepared to answer questions about things you do or what you believe and why.
16. Be quick to apologize when you make a mistake.
17. Forgive others.
18. Constantly ask yourself what Jesus would do in your situation.
19. Use extreme discretion in choosing entertainment options. Others are watching and following your example.
20. Watch how you dress. Reflect modesty. Don't provoke competition or temptation in others.
21. Be careful how you conduct yourself with the opposite sex. Your actions can make or break your witness.
22. Carry a Bible and read it in your spare time.
23. Wear a T-shirt with a Christian message.
24. Lend or give a CD from a Christian band to a friend.
25. Invite a friend who doesn't know Jesus to church.
26. Take a non-Christian friend to a Christian concert.
27. Host an event at your home with the purpose of inviting people who don't know Christ.
28. Give a Bible to a friend. Mark the Bible with the plan of salvation (see pages 62–63 in the student Field Manual).
29. Distribute tracts or other Christian literature in various public places (e.g., restaurants, rest areas).
30. Call or write a friend who is hurting. Offer to pray for him or her.
31. Visit church guests at least once a month.
32. Do not hesitate to talk about what your church or youth group is doing.
33. Invite non-Christian friends to events associated with school or church (e.g., camps, clubs, Bible studies).
34. When assigned a speech, book review, or other project, select a topic that reflects your faith and values.
35. Present a research paper from a biblical perspective.
36. Write a report on a Christian book or biography.
37. Be on time to class. Turn assignments in on time.
38. Give your best effort in school and in after-school activities.
39. Be polite.
40. Volunteer as a mentor or peer helper.
41. Help a struggling team member work on his or her game or practice for an extracurricular activity.
42. Be a tutor for someone who needs help with studies.
43. Volunteer to be a student manager for a sports team.
44. Volunteer to serve at school functions.
45. Volunteer to bring food for a sports team.
46. Organize students to serve during a crisis.
47. Help raise money for special needs.
48. Help organize a school assembly with a Christian speaker.
49. Run for a class or club officer position.
50. Invite the school choir to sing or the band to play at your church.
51. Perform a song or drama with a strong Christian message in a talent show.
52. Write a poem about your relationship with God.
53. Create a piece of art depicting your faith in Christ.
54. Write a verse next to your signature in others' yearbooks.
55. Offer to pray for your principal or other leaders.
56. Read a Christian book during breaks. Be ready to explain to people what you are reading and why.
57. Offer to show new students around school.
58. Each week hang a new memory verse in your locker.
59. Pray daily for opportunities to share Jesus with five non-Christian friends.
60. Look for opportunities to talk about God and spiritual matters.
61. Set a goal to share Jesus with one student each day.
62. Be a servant.
63. Volunteer your youth group to clean up after a football game.
64. Offer to help a new student find his or her way around school and town.
65. Invite your youth leader to eat lunch at school with you and your friends.
66. Ask your teacher if your youth leader can speak in class.
67. Send a teacher or coach a Christmas or birthday card.
68. Send thank-you cards to teachers, leaders, or other students whenever appropriate.
69. Organize a Teacher Appreciation Week.
70. Organize a special day to appreciate janitors and maintenance staff.
71. Give a coach a gift certificate to a restaurant.
72. Speak positively about others.
73. Attend or organize a campus Bible or prayer club.
74. Put an ad in your school paper for your Christian club.
75. Write an article or editorial for the school newspaper. Be gracious and noncombative.
76. Submit a picture with a caption of your Christian club to your yearbook staff.
77. Talk about what God is doing in your life.
78. Speak well of people. Don't be critical, but look for the best in others.
79. Offer to give another student a ride to school.
80. Offer to buy lunch for another student.
81. Sit by or eat lunch with someone who usually hangs out alone.
82. Be kind.
83. Visit someone who is sick or is a shut-in.
84. Ask a teacher or other student if there is anything you can pray about for him or her.
85. Play Christian music in classes when music is allowed.
86. Wash a friend's car.
87. Try doing random acts of kindness.
88. Set an example of good behavior in public, such as when you are at a restaurant with friends from church.
89. Become a generous tipper, especially if you discuss God at dinner or if you've just come from church.
90. Show respect for your parents.
91. Smile.
92. Open and hold doors for others.
93. Let others go first and have first choice.
94. Be nice to someone who is having a bad day.
95. Talk to everyone who walks into your youth group, regardless of appearance or actions.
96. Volunteer to do follow-up calls or visits to youth group guests.
97. Go on a mission trip. When you get back, show the pictures and talk about God.
98. Be generous and share with others.
99. Always give and do your best.

Adapted from the Campus Missions Training Helps in the *Fire Bible: Student Edition*. ©Life Publishers International, Springfield, Missouri, USA. Used by permission. All rights reserved.